C000173235

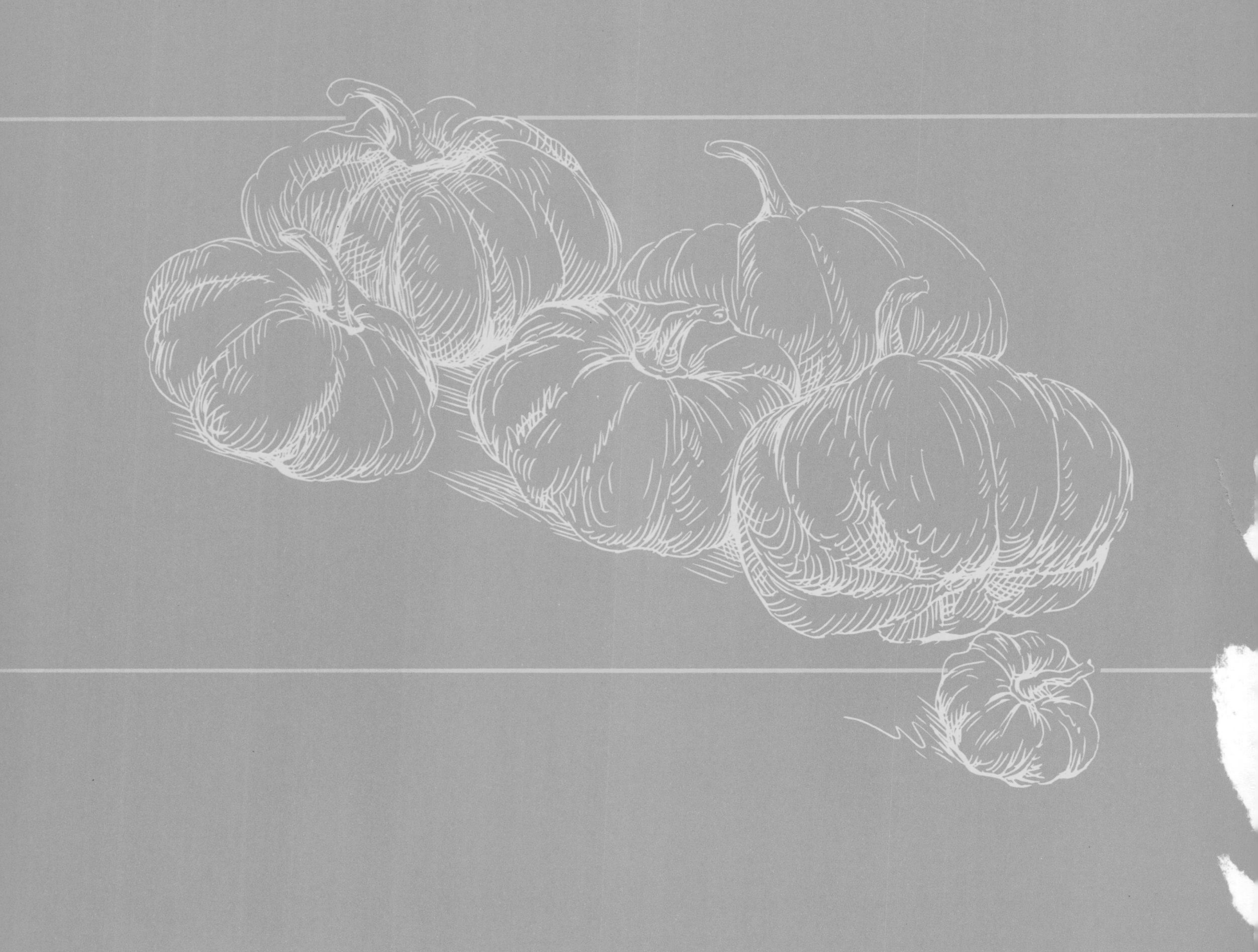

High fibre cookbook

High fibre cookbook

Reader's Digest

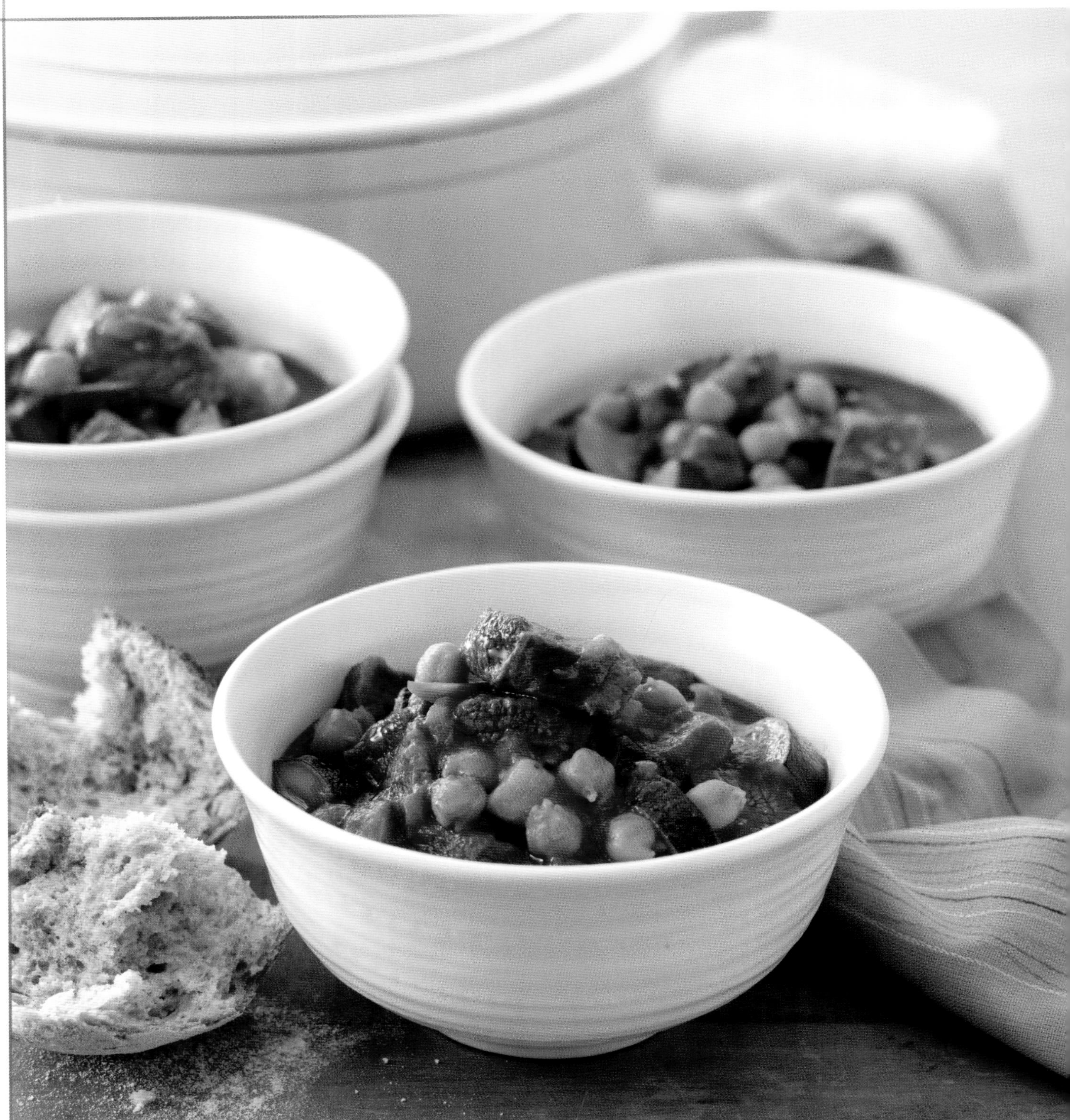

contents

All about fibre 8

The fibre fill-up 9

Good sources of dietary fibre 10

Grains 12

Beans, pulses & legumes 14

Breakfast & Brunch 16

Soups & Light Meals 42

Main Dishes 84

Salads 130

Side Dishes & Snacks 172

Desserts, Cakes & Breads 212

Index 250

Delicious recipes for a healthier you

Health experts the world over agree that today's ever-increasing reliance on packaged, packeted, processed, pulverised, frozen, canned, added-to, refined and 'improved' foods, has eliminated much of the wholesomeness from our diets.

As a result, most of us only consume half the dietary fibre that we need. Fibre is a simple substance that can reduce blood cholesterol, promote weight loss, reduce the risk of heart disease, assist with diabetes, and generally just make you feel more lively and energetic.

Many of the natural fibre foods from our past may be missing from the supermarket aisles but that doesn't mean that high-fibre cooking is difficult. Far from it! This cookbook proves that you don't have to start a strange diet or follow a special food regime to increase your fibre intake. The core of this book is the recipes, designed to ensure that eating the high-fibre way is never dull and always delicious. The satisfying, flavourful recipes provide quick and effortless ways to incorporate more fibre into every meal from breakfast, lunch and dinner, to desserts and snacks. They're really so tempting and delicious, you'll find it hard to believe that they're good for you too.

The Editors

All about fibre

Fibre is not actually a nutrient, since it is never absorbed by your body, so it may seem surprising that it is such a valuable component of your diet, with benefits ranging from heart health to diabetes and weight control.

What is fibre?

Fibre, simply put, is the stuff in plants that your body can't digest. It's the husks on the grains and the stringy threads in celery.

This fibre performs some vital functions in the body. There are two basic types of fibre: insoluble (insoluble in water) and soluble.

Insoluble fibre, which used to be known as roughage, helps move waste through the digestive tract by producing a bulkier, softer stool that stimulates the muscle movements of the bowel.

Some good sources of insoluble fibre are wheat bran and whole grains, the skins of apples and pears, and vegetables such as potatoes, carrots and broccoli

Soluble fibre is a gel-like substance that helps to thicken the stool. It may be broken down by gut bacteria to form beneficial substances. Soluble fibre is found in oats, barley, beans and many fruits and vegetables.

Different countries have different daily targets for fibre consumption, varying from 25 g to 38 g, but health experts agree it's a good idea generally to aim for about 30 grams per day.

Benefits of fibre

A high-fibre diet helps to prevent constipation, creating a soft stool that is easy to pass and moves through the gut more quickly. This may help to reduce the risk of colon cancer, as any toxins or carcinogens are diluted and spend less time in the bowel. Fibre encourages normal growth of the bowel cells too. Fibre feeds the beneficial bacteria that are naturally in the colon, discouraging harmful germs from growing there. The 'good' bacteria can break down the fibre to make butyrate, a short-chain fatty acid that acts as a gut tonic, providing energy to the bowel cells and helping to keep them healthy.

Fibre is also bulky and absorbs water so it fills you up fast. It also slows down digestion, prolonging feelings of fullness, which can help in maintaining a healthy weight.

Soluble fibre (such as that found in beans and lentils) has been shown to help to reduce cholesterol in your blood, protecting your heart. It also helps to keep blood glucose levels steady.

In addition to the known benefits of fibre itself, foods that are naturally high in fibre (foods from plant sources) tend to be rich in other important nutrients. See box on pages 10–11 for ways to add more fibre to your diet.

Fibre and the glycaemic index

The glycaemic index (GI) is a ranking of carbohydrate foods according to their effect on blood glucose levels. The theory is that the faster a food is broken down during digestion, the quicker the rise in blood glucose levels.High-fibre foods tend to take longer to eat, and the fibre stops the food from being quickly digested. Both of these factors help to reduce the glycaemic index (GI), so high-fibre foods tend to have a lower GI than their low-fibre equivalents. Another concept is the Glycaemic load (GL) which takes into account both the quality of carbohydrate (its GI) and the quantity in a food. A food's GL is the amount of carbohydrate in one serving, multiplied by the GI divided by 100. This represents an 'adjusted' value for the food's carbohydrate content. Although the GL is useful in scientific research, it is hard to apply to everyday food choices if serving sizes vary, so GI is a more helpful guide to choosing what to eat.

Foods that are fibre-rich tend to be more filling. Because the body does not absorb fibre, high-fibre foods are often also fairly low in kilojoules (calories) and so can help you to lose weight. Coupled with the fact that these foods can also help to control blood glucose and cholesterol levels, it makes sense to increase your fibre intake. Here's how:

Tips to increase your fibre

- Don't skimp on breakfast. A modest meal of whole grains and fruit provides as much as one-third of your daily fibre. Compare the fibre content of different breakfast cereals and choose those with more. A product with 6 g of fibre per serving is a good choice, though remember to check the fat and sugar content too. Muesli and porridge are good choices, as they contain lots of soluble fibre. Eat whole-grain bread instead of white bread and add chopped raw fruit to your cereal.

- Eat the skins. Scrub and eat the edible skins on fruits and vegetables rather than removing the peel. You lose about one-third of the fibre when you remove the skin from a potato. The seeds in berries, kiwifruit and figs also supply valuable fibre.

- Beans and lentils are a great source of fibre. Add beans to a salad, or fill a soft tortilla wrap with heated beans. Canned baked beans contain sugar, but are a good source of soluble fibre, so there's no need to opt for sugar-free varieties unless necessary.

- Add vegetables. Vegetables such as carrots and celery are good sources of fibre. Add them to casseroles, soups, salads, sandwiches and pasta dishes. Fresh, frozen, or even canned – all are good.

- Choose high-fibre snacks. Boost your daily fibre intake by choosing fruit instead of juice, popcorn instead of chips or crisps, fruitloaf instead of sponge cake. Nibble on dried fruit, nuts and seeds, or even some raw vegetable sticks. It all adds towards your 30 grams-a-day target.

- Switch from white to grainy bread. Buy whole-grain rather than wholemeal (whole-wheat) or white when choosing bread. Always check the labels because some so-called brown breads are actually not much higher in fibre than white bread. They get their brown look from colouring or molasses.

- Increase your fluid intake. When you eat more fibre, you need to make sure you are drinking sufficient amounts of fluid. Much of the benefit of fibre comes only when it absorbs plenty of water, like a sponge does. Without enough fluid, a high fibre intake can cause constipation.

GOOD SOURCES OF DIETARY FIBRE

Food	Amount	Dietary fibre (g)
CEREAL AND GRAIN FOODS		
Amaranth, cooked	½ cup (120 g)	2.6
Barley, pearl, cooked	½ cup (78 g)	2.7
Oat porridge (from rolled oats)	½ cup (120 g)	2.7
Oat porridge (from instant oats)	½ cup (120 g)	1.3
Quinoa, cooked	½ cup (95 g)	2.7
Rice, brown, cooked	½ cup (95 g)	1.5
Wheat bran	1 tablespoon	2.0
Wheatgerm	1 tablespoon	1.0
NUTS AND SEEDS		
Almonds, with skin	small handful (30 g)	3.5
Almonds, blanched	small handful (30 g)	2.7
Cashews	small handful (30 g)	1.8
Hazelnuts, with skin	small handful (30 g)	3.1
Macadamias	small handful (30 g)	1.8
Peanuts, raw with skins	small handful (30 g)	2.5
Peanuts, no skins	small handful (30 g)	1.9
Peanut butter	1 tablespoon	1.9
Sesame seeds	1 tablespoon (9 g)	0.9
Sunflower seed kernels	1 tablespoon (11 g)	1.2
Walnuts	small handful (30 g)	1.9
FRUITS		
Apple, with skin	1 medium (155 g)	3.6
Apple, peeled	1 medium (155 g)	1.7
Banana, fresh	1 medium (115 g)	3.2
Blueberries	½ punnet (100 g)	1.8
Figs, dried	3 figs	4.9
Figs, fresh	3 figs	4.9
Mango, fresh	1 small (300 g)	3.0
Orange, peeled	1 medium (140 g)	2.2
Peach, with skin	1 medium (150 g)	3.5
Pear, with skin	1 medium (185 g)	5.6
Plums	3 plums	4.0
Prunes	3 prunes	4.0
Raspberries	½ punnet (100 g)	3.1
Strawberries	½ punnet (125 g)	1.8
Sultana grapes	small bunch of 10 grapes (50 g)	1.2
Sultanas, dried	10 sultanas (1 tablespoon)	1.2

Food	Amount	Dietary fibre (g)
VEGETABLES AND LEGUMES		
Asparagus	5 spears (80 g)	1.8
Beans, baked	1 serving (100 g)	4.8
Beans, cannellini	1 serving (100 g)	6.4
Beans, kidney, cooked	1 serving (100 g)	6.5
Broad beans (fava beans)	1 serving (100 g)	7.6
Broccoli, cooked	½ cup (78 g)	3.0
Brussels sprouts, cooked	½ cup (78 g)	4.7
Cabbage, cooked	½ cup (73 g)	1.8
Carrot, cooked	1 medium (60 g)	1.7
Cauliflower, cooked	½ cup (62 g)	1.7
Celery	2 full-length stalks (80 g)	1.2
Corn	1 large cob	4.0
Lentils, cooked	1 serving (100 g)	3.7
Lettuce, finely-shredded	1 cup (72 g)	1.1
Peas, green, fresh, cooked	1 serving (100 g)	5.5
Peas, split, cooked	1 serving (100 g)	5.5
Potato with skin left on, boiled	1 large (185 g)	5.0
Potato, peeled, boiled	1 large (185 g)	4.0
Potato, instant mashed mixture	1 large serve (185 g)	3.0
Pumpkin	½ cup (123 g)	2.5
Radish, large white	½ large radish	1.9
Silverbeet greens, cooked	½ cup (72 g)	1.7
Snap or snow peas (edible pod)	½ cup (80 g)	2.2
Spinach, English, cooked	½ cup (90 g)	2.1
Tomato, raw	1 medium (123 g)	1.5
Turnip/swede	1 medium (122 g)	2.1

Grains

Grains – the family of cultivated botanical grasses – have been grown for food since the Stone Age. The earliest cereal-growing communities developed in the fertile lands of what are now Iraq, Turkey and Jordan. Today grains remain the 'staff of life'.

An ABC of grains

Different climates and growing conditions have given rise to different staple grains all over the world. This means an exciting range of grains can be used to bring variety, flavour and good nutrition to your table.

Barley Barley is rich in vitamins and iron, and has a low glycaemic index. Pot barley or barley groats, the whole grain of barley, contains much more dietary fibre, particularly soluble fibre, than any other cereal. Pot barley can be cooked in a similar way to rice as a side dish or to use in salads and pilafs. Pearl barley, made by removing the whole grain's outer layers, is most often used in soups and casseroles, as the starch in the grains acts as a thickener.

Buckwheat Buckwheat is high in protein and it also contains excellent amounts of fibre, vitamins, iron and calcium. Unroasted buckwheat grains are pale green-grey in colour and can be cooked like rice. Kasha is buckwheat groats that have been toasted, used to make a porridge of the same name. Kasha's toasty flavour is good with spicy dishes, and toasting your own is easy: just stir in a non-stick frypan over a medium heat until they turn light golden brown.

Maize Maize, or corn, can be harvested young as sweetcorn cobs or left to mature for a variety of uses such as cornflakes, popcorn, polenta or tortilla flour. Yellow corn contains antioxidant carotenes, and corn is generally a good source of iron and fibre, but it is lower in the other nutrients typical of most grains and some of the fibre is lost when corn is milled to produce hominy or polenta. Hominy and corn grits are American dishes that use dried white or yellow corn kernels either whole, broken or ground, which are then boiled in water or milk. Polenta can be cooked with water or stock until it thickens, then eaten soft, like a purée, or set and cut into shapes for baking or frying.

Millet This very small, golden cereal grain, native to Asia and Africa, has a delicate, slightly nutty flavour. It is a good source of fibre, protein and iron, and contains useful amounts of many of the B vitamins. In its wholegrain form, millet can be cooked in a similar way to other wholegrains. Sorghum is a larger relative of millet and can be used in similar ways.

Oats Oats are probably best known as porridge, usually made from rolled oats, which are whole oat grains that have been husked then flattened out while being steamed. Instant porridge or oatmeal is further milled, so it is lower in fibre and other nutrients. 'Steelcut' oats are flattened without heat. Rolled oats are great in baking, and whole oats grains (also known as kernels or groats) can be used like brown rice or pot barley. Oats (particularly whole oats or steel-cut oats) have a low glycaemic index, and are a good source of soluble fibre and beneficial fats, so are often recommended for cholesterol-lowering and heart health. Because oats contain more fat than other cereals, they can go rancid quickly if not kept refrigerated. The steaming process when they are rolled helps to preserve them.

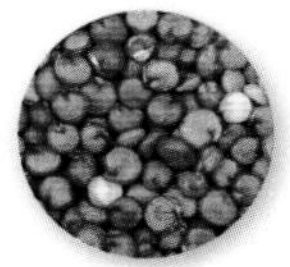

Quinoa Quinoa (pronounced 'keen-wah') is a small South American grain that comes in white, red and black varieties and is popular as a high-protein grain that is also high in fibre. It should be rinsed well before cooking, to remove the slightly bitter natural outer coating, and then boiled or steamed like the other wholegrains. It can be used like brown rice but has a slightly sweeter taste.

Rice Brown rice, red rice, coral rice, black rice and wild rice all have different flavours and can be used in similar ways. Rice flour is used across Asia for desserts, noodles and dumpling wrappers, and white rice is ubiquitous as the basis of a meal. But there are many whole-grain varieties that provide the additional benefits of fibre and higher levels of vitamins and minerals.

Rye Rye is perhaps the most important cereal crop in Scandinavia and parts of Central Europe, such as Russia and Germany, and is a hardy alternative to wheat, with a strong nutty flavour that enhances pumpernickel-type bread and crispbreads. Whole rye grains can be cooked like rice, but may take longer to cook. They are very tough when raw, so they need to be soaked overnight and then drained before cooking.

Spelt This is an ancient variety of wheat, from which our modern wheat was developed. Wholegrains of spelt can be cooked and used like rice. Spelt flour and spelt pasta are also available. Spelt is often higher in iron and B vitamins than modern wheat.

Wheat Ground into flour, wheat is the most popular grain for bread-making and pasta. White flour is produced by removing the wheat germ and the bran, the tough outer fibre layer of the grain. Bran is often used to supplement fibre in commercial products. Wheatgerm is rich in fibre and good fats, and needs to be refrigerated as it can go rancid. It can be sprinkled on foods such as breakfast cereal or salads. Pearled whole-wheat grains, or 'wheatberries', can be boiled and used in the same way as brown rice and other wholegrains. Kibbled or cracked wheat is made by milling pearled whole wheat so that it cooks more quickly than whole wheat. Bulgur wheat is also referred to as cracked wheat sometimes, but it is produced by cooking, and then drying, the wheat. This means that it needs only to be soaked before using.

Beans, pulses & legumes

When planning healthy meals, it's well worth making use of the family of pulses – also known as legumes – which include dried beans, peas and lentils. Being low in fat and high in dietary fibre, they have a lot to offer.

Why are legumes important?

Generally, grain legumes are referred to as pulses. They include beans, peas and lentils. Whether you call them legumes or pulses, they provide an excellent combination of protein and complex carbohydrate, without the undesirable fats often found in other protein foods. They are therefore an important source of protein for people trying to cut down their intake of animal and dairy fats, and for vegetarians and vegans. Most pulses do not provide all of the essential amino acids – the building blocks of protein – but eating them with pasta, rice or other grains makes up for this. The protein in pulses has a special role in protecting heart health, and the soluble fibre in pulses has been shown to lower cholesterol levels. Pulses are also a good source of insoluble fibre which is important for digestive health. Many pulses are good sources of B vitamins, including folate, and vitamin E. Pulses are key sources of iron, zinc and magnesium in vegetarian and vegan diets where meat – normally a main source of supply – is excluded.

An ABC of beans

There are hundreds of different varieties of dried beans throughout the world. Here is a selection of those that you are most likely to come across.

Adzuki bean Also spelled aduki or azuki, this is a very small, roundish, dark red bean with a slightly sweet taste. Popular in Japan, it is used in a variety of dishes, both savoury and sweet. Adzuki beans are higher in protein than many other pulses.

Black bean (Chinese) Not the black bean used in Mexican cooking, this medium-small, round, shiny black bean is a variety of soybean. It is fermented and salted, which gives it a rich savoury flavour. In Chinese cooking, fermented black beans are often mashed with a little sugar and water and added to dishes as a paste.

Black kidney bean Similar in shape and size to the red kidney bean, this has a black skin and a white flesh; it turns brown on cooking. Popular in Central and South America, black kidney beans are used to make the Brazilian national dish, feijoada.

Black-eyed bean Popular in Indian and Caribbean cooking as well as the Mediterranean, this is a pale, oval bean with a black 'eye'. It has a creamy texture with a slightly sweet flavour, and is good used in soups, stews and casseroles.

Borlotti bean This attractive bean is medium-sized, pale pink and speckled with brown. Being soft-textured it makes a creamy purée and is delicious in soups and salads. It comes from Italy and is sometimes called a cranberry bean.

Broad bean (fava bean) Also called faba bean, it can be bought dried, fresh or frozen. Large, flat and pale brown, with an earthy flavour, it is most often added to casseroles. Soak the dried beans before cooking.

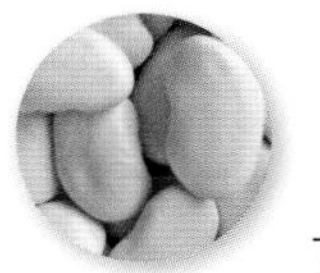

Butterbean (lima bean) From South America, this is a very large, flattish bean with an attractive deep cream colour. There is a hint of potato in the flavour. Butterbeans purée well and can be used as a side dish, dip or soup. Lima beans are used interchangeably as they are a close relation but slightly smaller.

Cannellini bean A variety of haricot bean grown widely in Italy, the cannellini is medium-large, cream-coloured and mild but pleasant in taste. Cannellini beans are good in soups, salads and casseroles, and go well in fish dishes, particularly those made with tuna.

Flageolet Popular in France and Italy, this is a medium-sized, pale green bean with a delicate yet distinctive flavour. It keeps its attractive colour when cooked, and is ideal in salads. If unavailable, use cannellini or navy beans.

Ful medames Also called Egyptian brown bean, this bean is small, round and mid-brown, with a full flavour, this is a variety of broad bean. It is native to Egypt where, combined with eggs, garlic and spices, it is made into the national dish of the same name. Ful medames are widely used in the Eastern Mediterranean.

Haricot bean This is the bean used for 'baked beans', so popular throughout the Western world – no wonder it is one of the most widely grown of all beans. Medium-sized and pale cream in colour, it is also the classic bean to use in a French cassoulet. Haricot beans contain more soluble fibre than any other pulse.

Pinto bean Looking like a borlotti bean but a little smaller, the pinto bean comes from Central and South America. With its creamy texture, it is good in soups and Mexican dishes. Use them cooked, mashed and fried for frijoles refritos.

Red kidney bean This red-skinned bean, with meaty white flesh, keeps its colour on cooking and absorbs other flavours well. Its robust taste and texture means it works well in hot, spicy dishes, such as chilli con carne. It is a good source of folate and dietary fibre.

Soybean Also referred to as soya beans, soybeans are much harder than other beans and need very long soaking and cooking. Soybeans are also quite bland, so need to be cooked with strongly flavoured ingredients, such as onion, tomato, spices or herbs. Soybeans provide a more 'complete' protein, as they contain the essential amino acids that are lacking in some other pulses.

Breakfast & Brunch

Bircher muesli

PREPARATION 10 minutes, plus overnight soaking   COOKING nil   SERVES 2

- 1/2 cup (50 g) rolled (porridge) oats
- 1/4 cup (30 g) sultanas (golden raisins)
- juice of 2 oranges
- 1/3 cup (50 g) almonds, roughly chopped
- 1 teaspoon ground cinnamon
- 1 large apple
- 1/2 cup (125 g) low-fat Greek-style yogurt, plus extra, to serve
- 200 g (7 oz) berries, to serve
- honey, to serve (optional)

Each serving provides
1532 kJ, 366 kcal, 11 g protein, 10 g fat (2 g saturated fat), 55 g carbohydrate (38 g sugars), 7 g fibre, 69 mg sodium

Combine the oats, sultanas and orange juice in a bowl and stir well to combine. Cover with plastic wrap and leave to soak in the refrigerator overnight.

Just before serving, stir in the almonds and cinnamon. Grate the apple (keeping the skin on) and discard the core. Stir the grated apple through the muesli mixture. Add the yogurt and fold through until evenly combined.

Divide the muesli between serving bowls, top with some berries and an extra dollop of yogurt, and drizzle over some honey, if desired.

Fibre fact

Coarse rolled oats are best for this recipe as quick-cooking instant varieties have less fibre and may become mushy after soaking. You can also vary the flavours by using other rolled whole grains, such as triticale or barley, and your choice of nuts and seasonal fruits.

Melon salad with lime & yogurt sauce

PREPARATION 20 minutes, plus chilling   COOKING nil   SERVES 8

Remove the skin and seeds from all of the melons and cut the flesh into bite-sized cubes. Gently toss in a large bowl with the grapes and pineapple, then cover and chill until serving time.

Combine the yogurt, sour cream, honey, lime juice and ginger in a small bowl. Mix well, then cover and chill until serving time.

Serve the fruit in individual bowls, with the lime and yogurt sauce on the side.

Fibre fact

The skins on the grapes add significant fibre to this dish, along with anti-oxidants that are protective against heart disease. The uniquely stringy texture of pineapple is due to its high insoluble fibre content. Pineapple also contains a protein-digesting enzyme, bromelain, which can react with foods such as jelly and yogurt to make them runny (this is why the yogurt sauce is served separately).

1/4 watermelon (about 1.5 kg/3 lb)

1/2 rockmelon (cantaloupe), (about 500 g/1 lb)

1/4 honeydew melon (about 250 g/8 oz)

1 cup (180 g) seedless red or green grapes

1 cup (160 g) fresh or canned pineapple pieces

Yogurt sauce

1 cup (250 g) low-fat natural (plain) yogurt

2 tablespoons low-fat sour cream

2 tablespoons honey

1 tablespoon lime juice

a pinch of ground ginger

Each serving provides
537 kJ, 128 kcal, 3 g protein, 1 g fat (<1 g saturated fat), 26 g carbohydrate (26 g sugars), 2 g fibre, 48 mg sodium

Winter fresh fruit salad

PREPARATION ***10 minutes*** *COOKING* ***30 minutes*** *SERVES 4*

$^{1}/_{3}$ cup (75 g) sugar

4 star anise

1 cinnamon stick

1 bay leaf

2 whole cardamom pods, squashed with the flat of a large knife

2 apples, cut into rounds (stem and seeds removed but skin left on)

2 pears, cut into rounds (stem and seeds removed but skin left on)

2 oranges, zest finely grated

low-fat Greek-style yogurt or whipped ricotta, to serve

Each serving provides
875 kJ, 209 kcal, 3 g protein, 2 g fat (<1 g saturated fat), 48 g carbohydrate (39 g sugars), 6 g fibre, 5 mg sodium

Preheat the oven to 200°C (400°F/Gas 6).

Put the sugar, star anise, cinnamon, bay leaf, cardamom pods and orange zest in a small saucepan with 1 cup (250 ml) water. Place over medium–low heat and simmer for 5 minutes.

Place the apple and pear slices in a large bowl and pour half the syrup over the top. Stir well to coat the fruit.

Arrange the apple and pear slices in a single layer in a baking tray and bake in the oven for 30 minutes, turning the fruit regularly and basting with the spice syrup, until the fruit turns golden and starts to caramelise.

Cut any white pith from the oranges and slice each orange carefully into 6 slices (collect any juice and add to the spice syrup). Remove any seeds and place the oranges in a large bowl.

Add the apple and pear slices to the bowl with the remaining spice syrup and stir to combine. Serve with the yogurt or ricotta on the side.

Fibre fact

This fruit salad is extra high in fibre thanks to the fruit skins and the way in which the fruit is cut, retaining the fibre (and concentrated anti-oxidants) found in their cores. Dried fruits such as apricots, dates and figs can be added to this recipe – just simmer them in the spice syrup to soften them, or soak in water beforehand (they do not need to be baked).

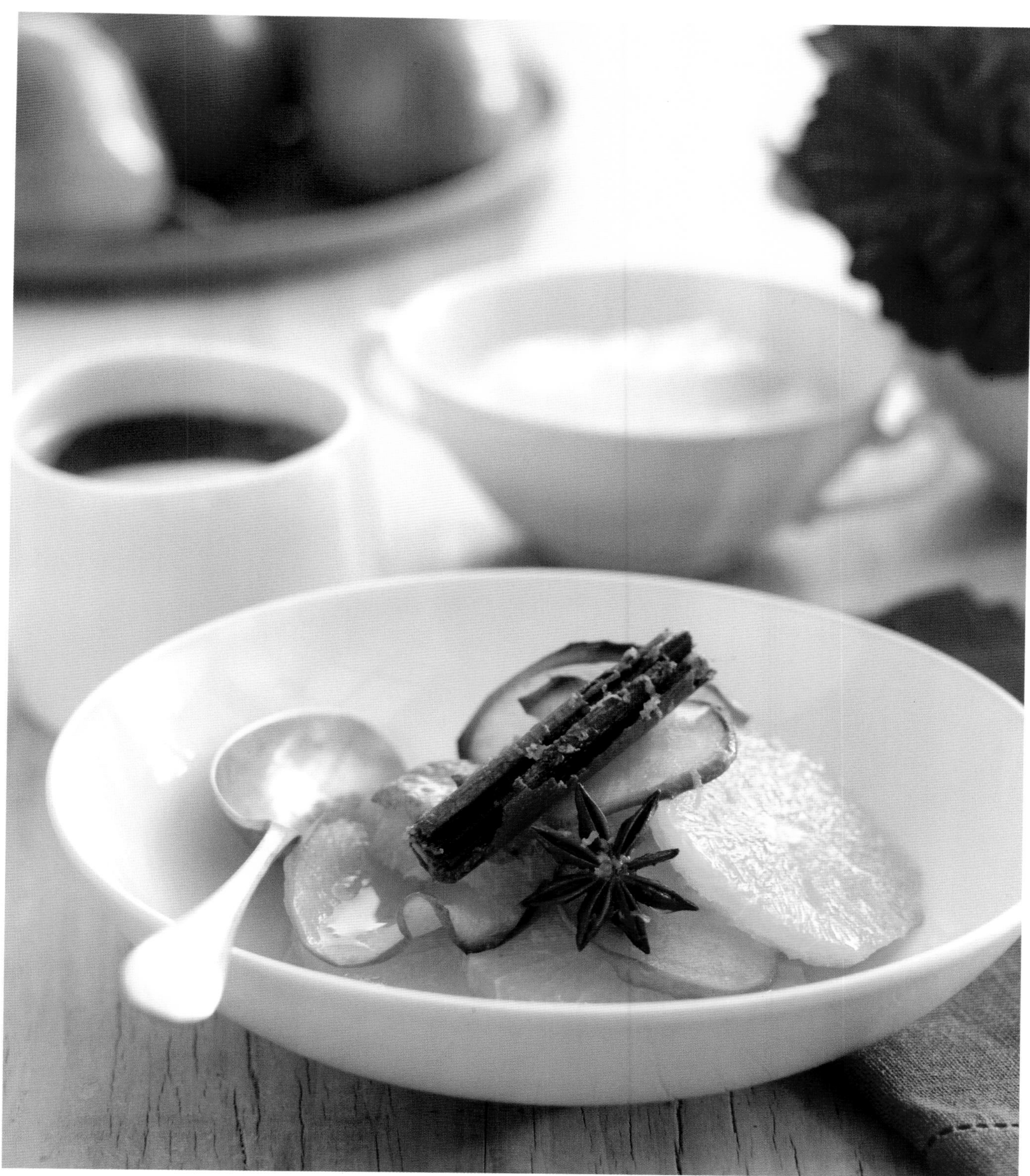

Fresh fruit muesli

PREPARATION 15 minutes, plus 30 minutes soaking COOKING nil SERVES 6

- 1/2 cup (90 g) burghul (bulgur)
- 3/4 cup (75 g) rolled (porridge) oats
- 1 cup (250 ml) apple juice
- 1/2 cup (60 g) slivered unblanched almonds
- 3 tablespoons pine nuts
- 2 tablespoons sunflower seeds
- 10 dried apricots, diced
- 10 dried figs, stalks removed, diced
- 1/3 cup (60 g) soft brown sugar
- 2 green apples, cored and coarsely grated
- 1 large or 2 small persimmons, peaches or nectarines, about 200 g (7 oz) in total, peeled and diced, plus extra, to garnish
- 1 passionfruit
- a few drops of almond extract (optional)
- pomegranate seeds or blueberries, to garnish

Put the burghul in a large bowl with 1 cup (250 ml) water and stir well to combine. Cover with plastic wrap and set aside for 30 minutes to soften. Drain well and return to the bowl.

Add the oats, apple juice, almonds and pine nuts to the burghul. Fold through the sunflower seeds, apricots, figs, sugar, grated apple and diced fruit until well combined.

Cut the passionfruit in half. Place a sieve over the bowl of muesli, spoon the passionfruit pulp and seeds into it, then press until the juice has passed through the sieve and only the seeds are left behind; discard the seeds.

Add the almond extract, if using, and a little more apple juice, if needed, to make a moist but not soggy consistency. Cover and refrigerate until required. Fresh fruit muesli will keep for up to 2 days, covered, in the refrigerator.

Stir the muesli well before serving and top with some pomegranate seeds or blueberries.

Fibre fact

A fibre powerhouse, this recipe contains many different types of soluble and insoluble fibres from grain, nut, seed and fruit sources, for a satisfying breakfast that provides long-lasting energy.

Each serving provides
1847 kJ, 441 kcal, 10 g protein, 16 g fat (2 g saturated fat), 65 g carbohydrate (42 g sugars), 14 g fibre, 29 mg sodium

Crunchy toasted cereal with fruit & nuts

PREPARATION 20 minute   COOKING 45–55 minutes   SERVES 10

3 tablespoons honey
$^{1}/_{3}$ cup (80 ml) apple juice
3$^{1}/_{3}$ cups (335 g) rolled (porridge) oats
3 tablespoons wheat flakes or extra (porridge) rolled oats
1$^{1}/_{3}$ cups (120 g) wheat germ
$^{2}/_{3}$ cup (60 g) flaked almonds
2 apples, halved, cored and thinly sliced or $^{2}/_{3}$ cup (50 g) dried apples
$^{1}/_{2}$ cup (60 g) raisins
$^{1}/_{2}$ cup (60 g) sunflower seeds

Each serving provides
1274 kJ, 304 kcal, 9 g protein, 11 g fat (2 g saturated fat), 41 g carbohydrate (18 g sugars), 7 g fibre, 11 mg sodium

Preheat the oven to 160°C (320°F/Gas 2–3). Put the honey and apple juice in a saucepan and stir well over medium heat until almost boiling, then remove from the heat and allow to cool.

Combine the oats, wheat flakes, wheat germ and almonds on a baking tray. Pour the honey mixture over the top and toss until the grains and nuts are evenly coated. Spread them out in an even layer and bake, stirring occasionally, for 30 minutes, or until toasted and golden brown. Remove from the oven and cool.

If using raw apples, reduce the oven temperature to 120°C (250°F/Gas $^{1}/_{4}$–$^{1}/_{2}$) and arrange the apple slices on two baking trays in a single layer. Dry the apple slices in the oven for 15–20 minutes, turning them once halfway through cooking. Allow to cool slightly, then chop the apples.

If using dried apples, chop them coarsely. Add the apples, raisins and sunflower seeds to the toasted grain mixture and mix well. Store the cereal in an airtight container in the refrigerator for up to 1 month. Serve with low-fat milk or low-fat natural (plain) yogurt.

Fibre fact

To increase the fibre in this recipe, use steel-cut or coarse rolled oats rather than quick (porridge) oats, and leave the skins on the apples before slicing them. You can use other rolled whole grains such as triticale, barley or rye for variety, and the apple can be replaced with other fruits.

Banana cinnamon muffins

PREPARATION 15 minutes COOKING 25 minutes MAKES 12 muffins

1 tablespoon raw (demerara) sugar
60 g (2 oz) oat bran
2 teaspoons ground cinnamon
3/4 cup (180 ml) soy milk
3 bananas
2/3 cup (125 g) soft brown sugar
1/4 cup (60 ml) sunflower oil
2 teaspoons natural vanilla extract
1 eggwhite
1 1/3 cups (200 g) wholemeal (whole-wheat) flour
1/2 cup (60 g) soy flour
1 tablespoon baking powder

Each serving provides
765 kJ, 182 kcal, 6 g protein, 6 g fat (1 g saturated fat), 26 g carbohydrate (13 g sugars), 4 g fibre, 69 mg sodium

Preheat the oven to 180°C (350°F/Gas 4). Line a 12-hole muffin tin with paper muffin cases.

Mix together the raw sugar, 2 teaspoons of the oat bran and 1 teaspoon of the cinnamon and reserve for the topping. Place the remaining oat bran in a small bowl with the soy milk and leave to soak for 5 minutes.

Roughly mash the bananas in a bowl. Add the brown sugar, oil, vanilla and eggwhite and beat together well.

Sift the flours, baking powder and remaining cinnamon into a large bowl. Make a well in the centre, then stir in the soaked oat bran and the banana. Mix lightly but thoroughly until just smooth.

Spoon the mixture into the paper cases and sprinkle with the topping. Bake for 20–25 minutes, or until the muffins are well risen and golden brown. Allow to cool slightly on a wire rack before serving.

Fibre fact

Oat bran is famous for its high soluble fibre content, making it beneficial for people concerned about their heart health. This recipe also provides heart-protective soy protein and minimises saturated fat by using eggwhites and oil instead of butter.

Breakfast bread pudding with berries

PREPARATION 10 minutes, plus 20 minutes standing COOKING 40 minutes SERVES 6

Place 2 tablespoons of the sugar in a bowl. Add the eggs, eggwhites, milk and vanilla and whisk together until combined.

Spray a 20 cm (8 inch) square baking dish with olive oil spray. Place four slices of toast in the bottom of the baking dish, then pour half the egg mixture evenly over the top. Repeat with the remaining toast and egg mixture. Allow to stand for 20 minutes.

Meanwhile, preheat the oven to 180°C (350°F/Gas 4). Place the baking dish in a large roasting pan. Set the roasting pan on an oven rack and pour in enough hot water to come halfway up the outside of the baking dish. Bake for 40 minutes, or until the pudding is set and the top is golden and puffed. Remove from the oven and allow to cool slightly.

In a bowl, toss the berries with the remaining sugar. Serve the pudding warm, topped with the berries.

Fibre fact

Berries are nutritionally very powerful, with an amazing fibre and anti-oxidant content for their size. Use frozen berries out of season.

1/4 cup (55 g) sugar
2 large eggs
3 large eggwhites
2 cups (500 ml) low-fat milk
1 teaspoon natural vanilla extract
olive oil spray, for greasing
8 slices wholemeal (whole-wheat) bread, toasted
2 cups (310 g) blueberries
2 cups (250 g) raspberries

Each serving provides
984 kJ, 235 kcal, 13 g protein, 3 g fat (1 g saturated fat), 37 g carbohydrate (23 g sugars), 6 g fibre, 299 mg sodium

Pear & rhubarb muffins

PREPARATION 10 minutes COOKING 30 minutes MAKES 12 muffins

Preheat the oven to 190°C (375°F/Gas 5). Line a 12-hole muffin tin with paper muffin cases.

Put the pears, rhubarb, milk, sugar, golden syrup and oil in a large saucepan. Bring to the boil, then reduce the heat to low and simmer for about 2 minutes, or until the rhubarb has softened – the mixture will look curdled but this is normal. Add the bicarbonate of soda and stir until frothy.

In a large bowl, combine the flours, oat bran, baking powder and spices and stir to combine. Pour the fruit mixture into the dry ingredients and stir gently until just combined. Spoon into the prepared muffin tin and bake in the oven for 30 minutes, or until the muffins are brown and risen. Allow to cool slightly on a wire rack before serving.

Fibre fact

The ingredients in these muffins provide a good blend of both soluble and insoluble fibres so that you get the health benefits of both kinds – they taste delicious too!

100 g (3½ oz) dried pears, cut into 5 mm (¼ inch) cubes, any tough parts removed

100 g (3½ oz) rhubarb stalks, trimmed and chopped into 1 cm (½ inch) lengths

1 cup (250 ml) low-fat milk

1 tablespoon soft brown sugar

2 tablespoons golden syrup or honey

2 tablespoons light olive oil

1 teaspoon bicarbonate of soda (baking soda)

⅔ cup (100 g) wholemeal (whole-wheat) flour

⅔ cup (100 g) self-raising flour

⅔ cup (100 g) oat bran

1 teaspoon baking powder

1 teaspoon ground cinnamon

1 teaspoon ground nutmeg

2 tablespoons ground ginger

Each serving provides
706 kJ, 169 kcal, 4 g protein, 4 g fat (1 g saturated fat), 29 g carbohydrate (10 g sugars), 4 g fibre, 260 mg sodium

Porridge with summer fruits

PREPARATION 5 minutes   COOKING 10 minutes   SERVES 2

1/2 cup (50 g) rolled (porridge) oats
1/3 cup (90 g) low-fat natural (plain) yogurt
1/2 cup (60 g) fresh raspberries
1/2 cup (80 g) fresh blueberries
2 teaspoons soft brown sugar

Each serving provides
648 kJ, 155 kcal, 5 g protein, 2 g fat (1 g saturated fat), 26 g carbohydrate (11 g sugars), 5 g fibre, 27 mg sodium

Place the oats and 2 cups (500 ml) of water in a small saucepan. Bring to the boil, then reduce the heat to low and simmer for 5 minutes, stirring regularly, until the oats have thickened and are cooked through.

Divide the porridge between two serving bowls and top each with 2 tablespoons of yogurt. Scatter the berries on top, then sprinkle each serve with a teaspoon of sugar.

Another idea

Use other fresh fruit if you prefer, such as sliced mangoes, apricots, peaches or nectarines.

Fibre fact

Oats contain a special type of soluble fibre called beta-glucan, which helps to bind cholesterol and remove it from the body. Beta-glucans work best when they are eaten as part of the whole oat grain, because then they can work together with other beneficial substances that oats provide. Both oats and berries contain heart-protective anti-oxidants as well.

Cinnamon French toast with sautéed apples

PREPARATION **15 minutes, plus 30 minutes soaking** *COOKING* **30 minutes** *SERVES* 4

1/2 cup (100 g) sugar
1 1/2 teaspoons ground cinnamon
2 eggs
1 1/4 cups (310 ml) low-fat milk
1 teaspoon natural vanilla extract
8 slices wholemeal (whole-wheat) or rye bread
1/2 cup (60 g) sultanas (golden raisins)
2 tablespoons butter
2 apples, peeled and thinly sliced
1/4 cup (60 ml) apple juice
1 tablespoon lemon juice

Each serving provides
2268 kJ, 542 kcal, 19 g protein, 16 g fat (7 g saturated fat), 77 g carbohydrate (56 g sugars), 13 g fibre, 378 mg sodium

Mix the sugar and cinnamon in a small bowl and set aside.

Whisk the eggs, milk, vanilla and 2 tablespoons of the cinnamon sugar in a large bowl. Working with one slice of bread at a time, dip into the egg mixture, coating both sides, then arrange in the base of a 33 x 23 cm (13 x 9 inch) baking dish so that each slice slightly overlaps. Cover with plastic wrap and refrigerate for at least 30 minutes, or up to 2 hours.

Preheat the oven to 190°C (375°F/Gas 5). Sprinkle the bread slices with another 2 tablespoons of the cinnamon sugar and bake for 30 minutes, or until the top of the French toast is browned and puffed.

Meanwhile, put the sultanas in a small saucepan with enough water to cover and gently cook for 5 minutes, or until soft and plump. Drain well.

Melt the butter in a large non-stick frying pan over medium heat. Add the apples and sauté for 4 minutes, or until golden brown and almost tender. Stir in the sultanas, apple juice and lemon juice, then sprinkle with the remaining cinnamon sugar. Cook for a further 3 minutes, or until the apples are tender but still hold their shape. Serve hot, with the French toast.

Fibre fact

To increase the fibre in this recipe, leave the skin on the apples. This helps them to hold their shape nicely once sautéed.

Eggs florentine

PREPARATION 15 minutes   COOKING 15 minutes   SERVES 2

- olive oil spray, for greasing
- 350 g (12 oz) English spinach leaves, trimmed
- freshly ground black pepper
- 2 large eggs
- 2/3 cup (150 ml) low-fat milk
- 1 tablespoon plain (all-purpose) flour
- 2 tablespoons grated low-fat cheddar
- 1 1/2 tablespoons grated parmesan
- 2 wholemeal (whole-wheat) English muffins, split and toasted

Each serving provides
1517 kJ, 362 kcal, 30 g protein, 13 g fat (5 g saturated fat), 32 g carbohydrate (7 g sugars), 8 g fibre, 618 mg sodium

Preheat the oven to 180°C (350°F/Gas 4). Grease a non-stick frying pan and two shallow gratin dishes (about 10 cm/4 inches in diameter) with olive oil spray.

Place the spinach in a large heatproof bowl and pour over enough boiling water to cover. Let stand for 2–3 minutes, or until soft, then drain well. When cool enough to handle, squeeze out the excess water and finely chop the leaves.

Season the spinach and divide between the gratin dishes to create a 'nest' in each dish, forming indentations with your fingers. One at a time, crack the eggs into a cup or small dish, then slide one egg into each spinach 'nest'. Bake for 15 minutes, or until the eggs are just set.

Meanwhile, put half of the milk and all the flour into a small jar with a tight-fitting lid; seal the jar and shake until well combined. Pour the mixture into a small saucepan over medium–high heat. Add the remaining milk and whisk constantly for 3 minutes, or until bubbles just form around the edge. Add the cheddar and parmesan and whisk for a further 4 minutes, or until the cheese has melted and the sauce is smooth.

Slide a spinach nest onto the bottom half of each toasted muffin and drizzle with the cheese sauce. Serve with the muffin tops.

Another idea

Instead of fresh spinach, you can chop and cook 250 g (8 oz) frozen spinach; thaw and squeeze dry before using.

Fibre fact

Spinach has twice as much fibre as most other vegetables, mostly the insoluble type. It is also high in the nutrients that help our bodies to use energy – great for an energetic start to the day.

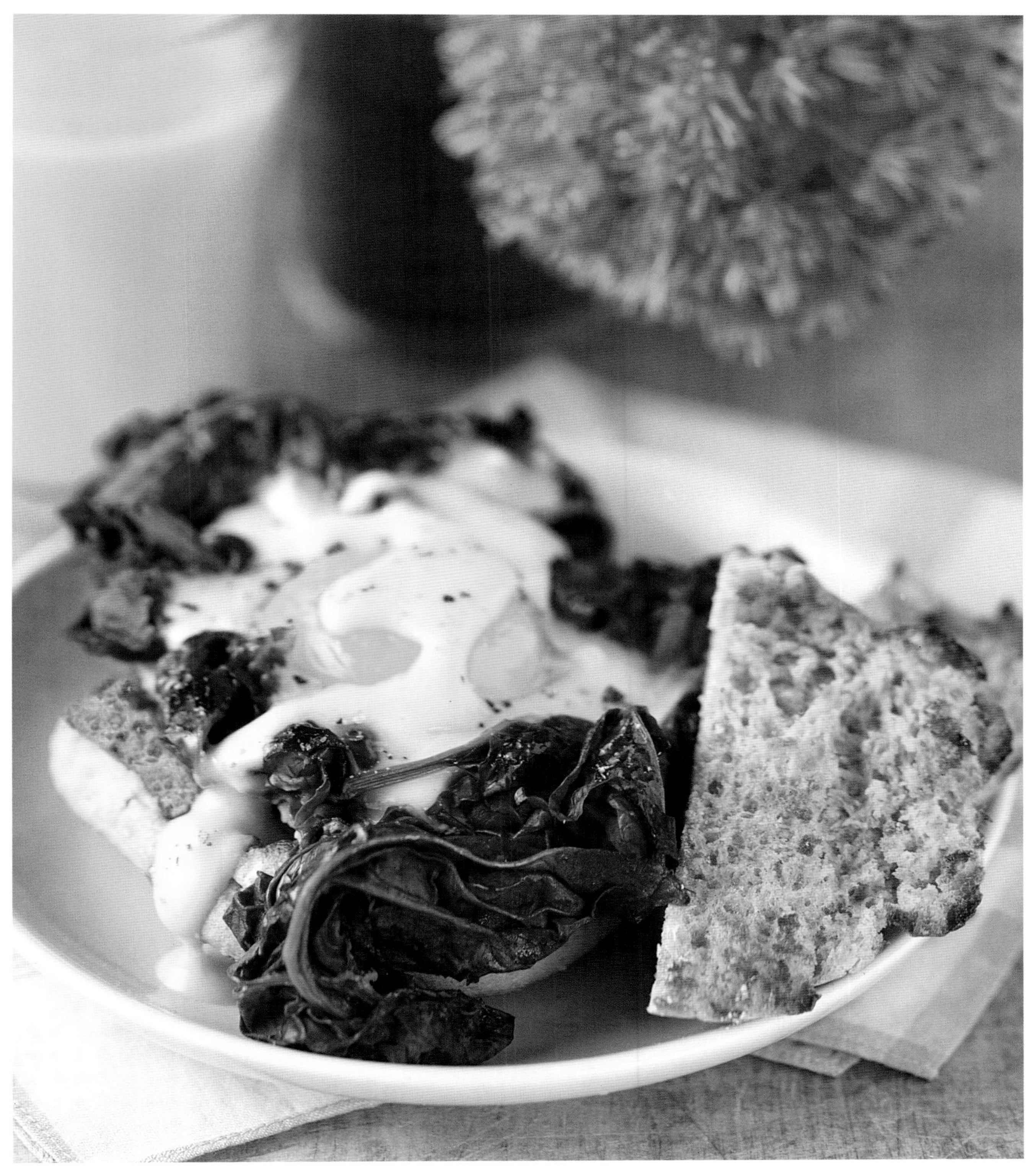

Mushroom & thyme toasts

PREPARATION **20 minutes** *COOKING* **5 minutes** *SERVES* 4

- 1/2 cup (125 g) low-fat ricotta
- 2 celery stalks, finely chopped
- 3 tablespoons finely chopped fresh parsley
- a good pinch of cayenne pepper
- 500 g (1 lb) chestnut or button mushrooms
- 1 clove garlic, crushed
- 2 tablespoons chopped fresh thyme
- 2 tablespoons low-fat sour cream
- 1 teaspoon lemon juice
- freshly ground black pepper
- 8 thick slices of mixed-seed bread, cut from a small loaf

Each serving provides
915 kJ, 218 kcal, 15 g protein, 9 g fat (5 g saturated fat), 16 g carbohydrate (2 g sugars), 10 g fibre, 217 mg sodium

Preheat the grill (broiler). In a bowl, mix together the ricotta, celery, parsley and cayenne pepper until combined. Set aside.

Leave any small mushrooms whole, halve any larger ones and place them all in a large non-stick frying pan over medium–low heat. Add the garlic, thyme, sour cream and 1 teaspoon water, then cover and cook for 3–4 minutes, or until the mushrooms are tender and have given up their juices. Add the lemon juice and season, to taste.

Meanwhile, toast the bread slices on both sides under the grill (broiler). While they are still warm, spread one side of each piece of toast with the ricotta mixture, then cut each piece in half.

Arrange the toasts on individual serving plates. Spoon the hot mushroom mixture over the toasts and serve immediately.

Fibre fact

Mushrooms are a valuable source of dietary fibre. A 100 g (3 1/2 oz) serve contains even more dietary fibre (2.5 g) than a slice of wholemeal (whole-wheat) bread (2 g).

Mixed greens frittata

PREPARATION ***15 minutes*** *COOKING* ***20 minutes*** *SERVES 4*

- 1 tablespoon olive oil
- 1 onion, chopped
- 2 cloves garlic, crushed
- 500 g (1 lb) mixed greens, such as kale, silverbeet (Swiss chard) and English spinach, washed, trimmed and torn into bite-sized pieces
- 2 eggs
- 4 eggwhites
- 1/4 cup (60 g) low-fat ricotta
- 3 tablespoons grated parmesan
- 3 teaspoons plain (all-purpose) flour

Heat half of the oil in a large non-stick frying pan with a heatproof handle over medium heat. Add the onion and garlic and cook for 2 minutes. Add the greens and cook, stirring often, for 7 minutes, or until wilted and tender. Remove to a plate and wipe the frying pan clean with paper towel.

Put the eggs, eggwhites, ricotta, parmesan and flour in a food processor. Process until well combined.

Preheat the grill (broiler). Heat the remaining oil in the frying pan over medium heat. Add the greens and the egg mixture, then cook without stirring for 10 minutes, or until the edges of the frittata are set but the centre is still slightly wobbly.

Transfer the frittata to the grill and cook for 1 minute, or until the centre is just set. Serve immediately.

Each serving provides
707 kJ, 169 kcal, 14 g protein, 11 g fat (3 g saturated fat), 4 g carbohydrate (2 g sugars), 4 g fibre, 223 mg sodium

Fibre fact

Green leafy vegetables are rich in valuable vitamins and minerals, and extremely high in fibre. You can vary the flavour of this dish by altering the greens you use, and even include some green leafy herbs such as basil or mint – both excellent fibre sources.

Spinach omelette & tomato mushroom sauce

PREPARATION ***10 minutes*** *COOKING* ***25 minutes*** *SERVES 2*

To make the tomato mushroom sauce, heat the olive oil in a small non-stick saucepan over medium–high heat. Add the mushrooms and cook for 4 minutes, or until softened. Add the tomato passata and simmer for 5 minutes, or until thickened. Remove from the heat and cover to keep warm.

To make the omelette, beat the eggwhites and egg in a small bowl and season well. Heat the olive oil in a large non-stick frying pan over medium heat. Add the onion and cook for 4 minutes, or until softened. Stir in the spinach and cook until heated through. Stir half the spinach mixture into the egg mixture and remove the rest to a plate.

Wipe out the frying pan and coat with olive oil spray. Reheat the pan over medium heat. Pour in the spinach and egg mixture, spreading it evenly. Cook without stirring for 1 minute, or until the omelette begins to thicken slightly around the edge. Run a thin spatula around the edge of the pan, lifting the mixture so the uncooked portion flows under the cooked egg. Cook for 3 minutes, or until the centre is still moist but not runny.

Spread the remaining spinach mixture over one half of the omelette; sprinkle with the parmesan. Fold the omelette over to cover the filling and reduce the heat to low. Cover and cook for 3–4 minutes, or until the egg is set but still soft. Slide the omelette onto a serving plate. Top with the tomato mushroom sauce and serve immediately.

Fibre fact

To increase the fibre in this recipe, make your own tomato sauce using fresh tomatoes. Cherry tomatoes make a deliciously sweet sauce and do not require peeling, so their skins and seeds add fibre and anti-oxidants. Simply fry some chopped onion and garlic in a small amount of olive oil until soft, then add a few handfuls of halved cherry tomatoes, simmering until the sauce has thickened.

Tomato mushroom sauce

1/2 teaspoons olive oil

125 g (4 oz) mushrooms, sliced

1 cup (250 ml) tomato passata (tomato purée)

Omelette

4 large eggwhites

1 large egg

freshly ground black pepper

1 teaspoon olive oil

1 small onion, chopped

2/3 cup (135 g) cooked chopped spinach (from about 150 g/5 oz fresh spinach)

olive oil spray, for cooking

2 teaspoons grated parmesan

Each serving provides
829 kJ, 198 kcal, 19 g protein, 8 g fat (2 g saturated fat), 12 g carbohydrate (10 g sugars), 6 g fibre, 633 mg sodium

Soups & Light Meals

Spiced cream of pumpkin soup

PREPARATION 15 minutes   COOKING 40 minutes   SERVES 4

- 2 teaspoons olive oil
- 1 large onion, finely chopped
- 4 red apples
- 1 kg (2 lb) butternut pumpkin (squash), peeled and thinly sliced
- 1 large all-purpose potato, peeled and thinly sliced
- 2 teaspoons curry powder
- 1 teaspoon ground ginger
- 1/2 teaspoon ground cinnamon
- 1 cup (250 ml) low-fat milk
- 1/4 cup (40 g) cashew nuts, roasted and coarsely chopped

Each serving provides
1465 kJ, 350 kcal, 10 g protein, 7 g fat (1 g saturated fat), 66 g carbohydrate (29 g sugars), 10 g fibre, 58 mg sodium

Heat the olive oil in a large saucepan over medium heat. Add the onion and cook for 8–10 minutes, stirring frequently, until golden brown.

Peel, core and slice 3 1/2 of the apples, reserving the remaining apple, unpeeled, to use as a garnish. Add the sliced apple to pan along with the pumpkin, potato, curry powder, ginger and cinnamon, stirring well to combine. Add 3 cups (750 ml) water; cover and simmer for 30 minutes, or until the pumpkin is tender.

Allow to cool slightly then transfer the mixture to a food processor and process until smooth. Return the mixture to the pan, add the milk and whisk well to combine. Continue to cook over low heat until heated through.

Meanwhile, thinly slice remaining apple. Divide the soup among mugs or serving bowls and top with the cashew nuts and some apple slices.

Fibre fact

Apples may seem like a surprising ingredient for a soup, but their sweetness gives depth of flavour to this dish and they add valuable fibre and anti-oxidants. The garnish of cashew nuts and unpeeled apple slices boosts the fibre content even further.

Red lentil & celery soup

PREPARATION 15 minutes   COOKING 45 minutes   SERVES 4

Heat the olive oil in a large saucepan over low heat. Add the onion and cook, stirring occasionally, for 5–7 minutes, or until it softens.

Tip the lentils into the pan and add the vegetable stock and 5 cups (1.25 litres) water. Bring to the boil, then add the carrots and celery. Bring back to the boil, cover, and simmer for about 40 minutes, or until the lentils and vegetables are very tender.

Allow to cool slightly then transfer the mixture to a food processor and process until smooth. Return the mixture to the pan and continue to cook over low heat until heated through. Remove the pan from the heat and stir in the blue cheese and chives.

Divide the soup among serving bowls, season, to taste, and garnish with the reserved celery leaves; serve hot.

Fibre fact

Lentils are a good source of fibre, protein, starchy carbohydrate and B vitamins. Unlike other lentils, red lentils do not need to be soaked before cooking.

1 1/2 tablespoons extra virgin olive oil

1 large onion, roughly chopped

1 1/2 cups (375 g) split red lentils

2 cups (500 ml) salt-reduced vegetable stock

4 large carrots, sliced

500 g (1 lb) celery stalks, sliced, some of the leaves reserved for garnish

1/3 cup (40 g) crumbled blue cheese

1/3 cup (10 g) snipped fresh chives

freshly ground black pepper

Each serving provides
1490 kJ, 356 kcal, 22 g protein, 13 g fat (4 g saturated fat), 39 g carbohydrate (10 g sugars), 15 g fibre, 800 mg sodium

Split pea & green pea soup

PREPARATION 15 minutes   COOKING 35 minutes   SERVES 4

1 tablespoon vegetable oil
6 spring onions (scallions), sliced
3 cloves garlic, crushed
4 cups (1 litre) salt-reduced chicken or vegetable stock
1¼ cups (275 g) split peas
⅓ cup (10 g) fresh mint
1 teaspoon fresh marjoram
1½ cups (195 g) frozen green peas
1 tablespoon low-fat natural (plain) yogurt
freshly ground black pepper

Each serving provides
1170 kJ, 279 kcal, 19 g protein, 5 g fat (1 g saturated fat), 40 g carbohydrate (8 g sugars), 8 g fibre, 1380 mg sodium

Heat the vegetable oil in a large saucepan over medium heat. Add the spring onions and garlic and cook for 2 minutes, or until tender. Add the stock, split peas and herbs and bring to the boil. Reduce the heat, cover, and simmer for 25 minutes.

Stir in the green peas and cook for a further 5 minutes, or until the split peas and the green peas are tender. Allow to cool slightly then transfer the mixture to a food processor and process until smooth. Return to the pan and continue to cook over low heat until heated through.

Divide the soup among serving bowls and swirl 1 teaspoon yogurt into each bowl; season, to taste.

Fibre fact

Split peas are full of soluble fibre. One cup of cooked split peas contains over 65 per cent of the recommended daily fibre intake.

Celeriac & spinach soup

PREPARATION 15 minutes   COOKING 20 minutes   SERVES 4

2 tablespoons extra virgin olive oil
1 large onion, thinly sliced
1 clove garlic, crushed
500 g (1 lb) celeriac, peeled and grated
4 cups (1 litre) salt-reduced vegetable stock
500 g (1 lb) baby spinach leaves
freshly grated nutmeg, to taste
freshly ground black pepper
$^1/_3$ cup (90 g) low-fat natural (plain) yogurt
fresh chives, to garnish

Heat the olive oil in a large saucepan over low heat. Add the onion and garlic and cook for 5 minutes, or until the onion has softened. Add the celeriac and stock and bring to the boil, then reduce the heat to low, cover, and simmer for 10 minutes, or until the celeriac is tender.

Add the spinach to the pan and stir well. Bring back to the boil, then remove the pan from the heat. Allow to cool slightly, then transfer to a food processor and process until smooth – the soup will still be fairly thick. Return to the pan and continue to cook over low heat until heated through.

Just before serving, stir in a little grated nutmeg and season, to taste. Divide the soup among serving bowls, swirl a spoonful of yogurt over each portion and garnish with fresh chives.

Each serving provides
770 kJ, 184 kcal, 7 g protein, 13g fat (1 g saturated fat), 10 g carbohydrate (8 g sugars), 10 g fibre, 253 mg sodium

Fibre fact

Celeriac is a wonderful ingredient for soups, providing a savoury celery flavour along with a creamy colour and silky consistency that works well with a variety of other ingredients. In this case, celeriac's moderate fibre content is boosted with the addition of high-fibre spinach. You can vary this dish by combining different vegetables with the celeriac.

Mediterranean roasted vegetable soup

PREPARATION ***25 minutes*** *COOKING* ***40 minutes*** *SERVES 4*

1 tablespoon olive oil

5 cloves garlic

350 g (12 oz) all-purpose potatoes, such as desiree, unpeeled and diced

1 green capsicum (bell pepper), seeded and diced

1 yellow capsicum (bell pepper), seeded and diced

1/2 teaspoon fresh rosemary, chopped

1 zucchini (courgette), halved lengthwise and cut into 1 cm (1/2 inch) pieces

1 red onion, cut into 1 cm (1/2 inch) chunks

1 1/2 cups (375 ml) carrot juice

375 g (3/4 lb) roma (plum) tomatoes, diced

1 teaspoon fresh tarragon

Each serving provides
703 kJ, 168 kcal, 6 g protein, 5 g fat (1 g saturated fat), 24 g carbohydrate (11 g sugars), 6g fibre, 59 mg sodium

Preheat the oven to 230°C (450°F/Gas 8). Combine the olive oil and garlic in a roasting pan and roast until the oil begins to sizzle, about 5 minutes. Add the potatoes, capsicums and rosemary, and toss to coat in the oil and garlic. Roast for about 15 minutes, or until the potatoes begin to colour and soften. Add the zucchini and onion and roast until the zucchini is tender, about 15 minutes.

Put the carrot juice, tomatoes and tarragon in a saucepan and bring to the boil. Spoon the roasted vegetables into the saucepan and mix well to combine.

Pour a little water into the roasting pan and stir, making sure to scrape up any browned bits that stick to the base of the pan. Pour the pan juices into the saucepan and continue to cook for about 2 minutes, or until heated through. Divide the soup among serving bowls and serve hot.

Fibre fact

The deeply coloured vegetables in this soup are not only high in fibre but contain a wide spectrum of nutrients. You'll also benefit from a number of potent, disease-fighting carotenoids, such as beta-carotene and lycopene.

Mushroom & winter vegetable soup

PREPARATION ***20 minutes, plus 15 minutes soaking*** *COOKING* ***40 minutes*** *SERVES 4*

If using dried mushrooms, put the mushrooms in a small bowl, then cover with 1 1/2 cups (375 ml) boiling water. Let them stand for 15 minutes, or until rehydrated and softened. Remove the mushrooms from the soaking liquid with a slotted spoon, reserving the liquid. Trim and discard any tough stems from the mushrooms and roughly chop the caps. Strain the reserved liquid through a sieve and set aside.

Meanwhile, heat the olive oil in a large saucepan over medium heat. Add the onion and garlic and cook for about 5 minutes, stirring occasionally until the onion softens. Add the carrot and parsnip and cook for 5 minutes, then stir in the cabbage. Cover and cook for a further 5 minutes, or until the cabbage begins to wilt.

Stir in the mushrooms and the reserved soaking liquid, the beans, tomato paste, vinegar, dill and 3 cups (750 ml) water. Bring to the boil, then reduce the heat to low, cover and simmer for 25 minutes, or until well flavoured; season, to taste.

Another idea

You can vary this soup by adding other varieties of canned beans, such as red kidney or cannellini beans.

Fibre fact

The vegetables in this soup have amazing levels of anti-oxidants, which can help keep you healthy through winter. Cabbage is one of the highest-fibre vegetables and is combined here with other high-fibre ingredients such as carrots and parsnip.

1/2 cup (10–15 g) dried shiitake or porcini mushrooms or 150 g (5 oz) fresh cultivated mushrooms

2 tablespoons olive oil

1 large onion, finely chopped

4 cloves garlic, crushed

1 large carrot, thinly sliced

1 large parsnip, thinly sliced

1 small head green cabbage, shredded (about 8 cups/400 g)

1 1/4 cups (220 g) frozen baby lima beans or broad (fava) beans, thawed

1/3 cup (90 g) tomato paste (concentrated purée)

1/4 cup (60 ml) red wine vinegar

1/3 cup (10 g) chopped fresh dill or 1 teaspoon dried dill (optional)

freshly ground black pepper

Each serving provides
1050 kJ, 251 kcal, 9 g protein, 10 g fat (1 g saturated fat), 31 g carbohydrate (14 g sugars), 13 g fibre, 340 mg sodium

Chunky vegetable soup

PREPARATION 15 minutes   COOKING 1 hour   SERVES 4

1 tablespoon canola oil
1 small onion, chopped
1 small leek, white part only, thinly sliced
1 large carrot, thinly sliced
1 fennel bulb, sliced, leaves reserved to garnish
250 g (8 oz) swede (rutabaga), peeled and cut into cubes
250 g (8 oz) all-purpose potatoes, peeled and cut into cubes
1 bay leaf
a few sprigs of fresh thyme
a few sprigs of fresh flat-leaf parsley
2 1/3 cups (600 ml) salt-reduced vegetable stock
410 g (15 oz) can chopped tomatoes
freshly ground black pepper

Each serving provides
690 kJ, 165 kcal, 5 g protein, 6 g fat (< 1 g saturated fat), 24 g carbohydrate (13 g sugars), 7 g fibre, 727 mg sodium

Heat the canola oil in a large saucepan over medium heat. Add the onion and cook for about 5 minutes, stirring occasionally, or until the onion has softened.

Add the leek, carrot, fennel, swede and potatoes, and cook for 5 minutes, or until slightly softened. Tie the bay leaf, thyme and parsley sprigs together into a bouquet garni. Add to the pan, together with the stock and tomatoes; season, to taste. Bring to the boil, then reduce the heat to low, cover, and simmer for 45 minutes, or until all the vegetables are tender.

Remove the bouquet garni and check the seasoning. Divide the soup among serving bowls and sprinkle over some snipped fennel leaves before serving.

Another idea

For a hearty winter's chowder-type soup, simply add more vegetables. Try celeriac, turnips and parsnips. Shredded white or green cabbage is also good – add green cabbage halfway through simmering. Cool and chill any leftovers and reheat them the next day, when the soup will taste even more flavoursome.

Fibre fact

Fennel is a great source of fibre, and in this recipe it is combined with a variety of hearty root vegetables. To increase the fibre content of this recipe, leave the skin on the carrot and potato cubes – this will boost the soup's anti-oxidant content as well.

Mixed bean chilli soup

PREPARATION 20 minutes COOKING 25 minutes SERVES 4

Heat the vegetable oil in a large saucepan over medium heat. Add the onion, garlic and capsicums and cook for 5 minutes, stirring constantly until softened. Add the mushrooms, chilli powder and cumin and cook for about 30 seconds, stirring to coat the vegetables.

Add the beans, tomatoes and tomato juice to the pan with the stock and coriander. Stir well, bring to the boil, then reduce the heat to low, partially cover the pan, and simmer for 20 minutes, or until the vegetables are tender.

Divide the soup among serving bowls and garnish each with a dollop of sour cream and a coriander sprig.

Another idea

A 750 g (1 1/2 lb) jar of tomato passata (puréed tomatoes) could be used instead of the combined canned tomatoes and tomato juice, with a little extra stock as needed.

Fibre fact

Providing both protein and fibre as well as being rich in vitamins and minerals, the legume family is known as one of the world's true 'wonder foods'. The peas, beans and lentils in this family contain a variety of soluble and insoluble fibres as well as resistant starch, making them a satisfying source of long-lasting energy.

2 tablespoons vegetable oil

1 onion, chopped

2 cloves garlic, crushed

1 red capsicum (bell pepper), seeded and chopped

1 green capsicum (bell pepper), seeded and chopped

3/4 cup (65 g) sliced button mushrooms

1/2 teaspoon chilli powder, or to taste

1 teaspoon ground cumin

410 g (15 oz) can mixed beans, rinsed and drained

410 g (15 oz) can chopped tomatoes

2 cups (500 ml) tomato juice

1 cup (250 ml) salt-reduced vegetable stock

2 tablespoons chopped fresh coriander (cilantro) leaves

1/3 cup (90 g) low-fat sour cream or low-fat Greek-style yogurt

4 sprigs fresh coriander (cilantro), to serve

Each serving provides
1004 kJ, 240 kcal, 9 g protein, 13 g fat (3 g saturated fat), 21 g carbohydrate (12 g sugars), 8 g fibre, 901 mg sodium

Chicken & soba noodles

PREPARATION ***20 minutes*** *COOKING* ***15 minutes*** *SERVES* ***4***

- 3/4 cup (180 ml) salt-reduced chicken stock
- 2 cloves garlic, crushed
- 1/2 teaspoon ground ginger
- 1/4 teaspoon dried red chilli flakes
- 375 g (3/4 lb) skinless, boneless chicken breasts
- 300 g (10 oz) soba noodles (buckwheat noodles)
- 250 g (8 oz) green beans, halved
- 2 carrots, cut into matchsticks
- 1 1/2 tablespoons dark brown sugar
- 1 tablespoon salt-reduced soy sauce
- 1 tablespoon peanut or other vegetable oil
- 2 cups (150 g) finely shredded cabbage

Each serving provides
2003 kJ, 479 kcal, 32 g protein, 10 g fat (2 g saturated fat), 62 g carbohydrate (9 g sugars), 7 g fibre, 1142 mg sodium

Put the stock, garlic, ginger and chilli flakes into a large non-stick frying pan and bring to the boil. Reduce the heat to low, add the chicken, cover, and simmer for 5 minutes. Turn the chicken over and cook for a further 5 minutes, or until cooked through. Remove the chicken to a plate, reserving the cooking liquid. When it is cool enough to handle, shred the chicken.

Meanwhile, cook the noodles in a large saucepan of boiling water according to the packet instructions. Blanch the beans and carrots for the last minute of cooking time until just tender. Drain well.

Whisk together the sugar, soy sauce, peanut oil and the reserved cooking liquid in a large bowl. Add the shredded chicken, noodles, beans, carrots and the cabbage, tossing to combine. Divide among serving bowls and serve the noodles at room temperature or chilled.

Fibre fact

Buckwheat, from which soba noodles are made, is not a true grain; it is the fruit of a rhubarb-like plant. It is a rich source of dietary fibre, is gluten-free and also contains more lysine – an essential amino acid – than other grains.

Spaghetti with spicy tomato sauce

PREPARATION ***10 minutes*** *COOKING* ***25 minutes*** *SERVES 4*

- 2 tablespoons olive oil
- 1 onion, chopped
- 1 clove garlic, crushed
- 1 celery stalk, finely chopped
- 410 g (15 oz) can chopped tomatoes
- 2 x 410 g (15 oz) cans chickpeas, rinsed and drained
- 1/2 teaspoon Tabasco sauce, or to taste
- 200 g (7 oz) baby spinach leaves
- freshly ground black pepper
- 350 g (12 oz) wholemeal (whole-wheat) spaghetti
- 1/2 cup (45 g) grated pecorino cheese, to serve
- fresh flat-leaf parsley, to garnish

Heat the olive oil in a heavy-based saucepan over medium heat. Add the onion and garlic and cook for 5 minutes, or until softened. Add the celery and cook for 1–2 minutes, stirring occasionally, then add the tomatoes and bring to the boil. Reduce the heat to low and simmer for about 15 minutes, stirring regularly, until the sauce has thickened.

Stir the chickpeas and Tabasco into the tomato sauce. Add the spinach and simmer, stirring, for 1–2 minutes or until the spinach wilts; season, to taste.

Meanwhile, cook the spaghetti in a large saucepan of boiling water according to the packet instructions. Drain well.

Toss the spaghetti with the tomato sauce mixture. Divide among serving bowls and serve immediately, sprinkled with the pecorino cheese and parsley.

Each serving provides
2354 kJ, 562 kcal, 25 g protein, 18 g fat (4 g saturated fat), 75 g carbohydrate (5 g sugars), 17 g fibre, 493 mg sodium

Fibre fact

Despite its name, the chickpea is not really a pea but a bean. Chickpeas are part of the classification of vegetables that includes peas, lentils and beans. Chickpeas are also known as garbanzo beans. They are high in fibre and have a low glycaemic index, making them an excellent food for weight loss.

Spaghetti with artichokes & broad beans

PREPARATION **10 minutes** *COOKING* **10 minutes** *SERVES* 4

- 400 g (14 oz) spelt spaghetti
- 250 g (8 oz) frozen broad (fava) beans, defrosted
- 400 g (14 oz) bottled artichoke hearts, drained
- 1/3 cup (50 g) chopped semi-dried tomatoes
- 1/4 cup (60 g) pesto
- freshly ground black pepper
- grated parmesan, to serve

Each serving provides
1983 kJ, 474 kcal, 22 g protein, 13 g fat (2 g saturated fat), 65 g carbohydrate (3 g sugars), 15 g fibre, 362 mg sodium

Cook the spaghetti in a large saucepan of boiling water according to the packet instructions.

To peel the broad beans, use your fingertips to split the skin at one end of the bean. Squeeze gently to remove the bean. Discard the skin. Add the peeled broad beans during the final 5 minutes of cooking the spaghetti. Drain well, reserving 1/3 cup (80 ml) of the cooking liquid.

Meanwhile, cut each artichoke heart into six pieces. Transfer the spaghetti and beans to a large serving bowl. Add the artichoke hearts and tomatoes.

Combine the pesto with the reserved cooking liquid and spoon over the spaghetti mixture. Season, to taste, then toss gently to combine. Serve immediately with the parmesan on the side for guests to help themselves.

Another idea

You can substitute wholemeal (whole-wheat) pasta if spelt pasta is not available.

Fibre fact

Spelt is one of the oldest cultivated grains – an ancient cousin of wheat – and has a naturally mild flavour. It is high in fibre, and has a higher content of protein and vitamins than wheat.

Pasta with roasted asparagus

PREPARATION 10 minutes COOKING 10 minutes SERVES 4

Preheat the oven to 230°C (450°F/Gas 8). Toss together the asparagus, corn and olive oil in a 33 x 22 cm (13 x 8 1/2 inch) baking dish. Bake for 10 minutes, or until the asparagus is tender and lightly browned.

Meanwhile, cook the spaghetti in a large saucepan of boiling water according to the packet instructions. Drain well, reserving 1 cup (250 ml) of the cooking liquid.

Transfer the pasta to a large bowl and add the asparagus and corn. Pour over the reserved cooking liquid, add the parmesan, goat's cheese and parsley, and toss well to combine; season, to taste. Divide the pasta among serving bowls and serve with the walnuts sprinkled over the top.

Fibre fact

Asparagus has been enjoyed since ancient times, and is valued for its medicinal properties as well as its fibre and folate content. In this recipe, other high-fibre ingredients such as walnuts, corn kernels and wholemeal (whole-wheat) pasta combine with asparagus to make a colourful and tasty high-fibre dish.

750 g (1 1/2 lb) asparagus, cut into 3 cm (1 1/4 inch) lengths

1 1/2 cups (225 g) frozen corn kernels or kernels from 3 corn cobs

1 tablespoon olive oil

250 g (8 oz) wholemeal (whole-wheat) spaghetti or spaghettini

1/4 cup (25 g) grated parmesan

1/2 cup (60 g) crumbled soft goat's cheese

2 tablespoons chopped fresh flat-leaf parsley

freshly ground black pepper

1/4 cup (25 g) walnuts, roasted and chopped

Each serving provides
1893 kJ, 452 kcal, 20 g protein, 18 g fat (5 g saturated fat), 51 g carbohydrate (5 g sugars), 11 g fibre, 165 mg sodium

Grilled polenta & tuna pizza

PREPARATION **10 minutes** *COOKING* **25 minutes** *SERVES* 4

350 g (12 oz) instant polenta

1 tablespoon chopped fresh thyme, plus extra, to garnish

3 tablespoons chopped fresh flat-leaf parsley

freshly ground black pepper

1 tablespoon extra virgin olive oil

410 g (15 oz) can chopped tomatoes

1 yellow capsicum (bell pepper), halved and seeded

200 g (7 oz) can tuna in springwater, drained and flaked

250 g (8 oz) low-fat ricotta

12 pitted black olives, halved

Each serving provides
2114 kJ, 505 kcal, 25 g protein, 15 g fat (5 g saturated fat), 67 g carbohydrate (6 g sugars), 4 g fibre, 365 mg sodium

Put the polenta in a large saucepan with 5 cups (1.25 litres) water and cook according to the packet instructions, until thick and smooth. Remove from the heat and stir in the thyme and parsley; season, to taste. Spoon the polenta onto a greased baking tray or pizza tray and spread out to make a smooth 30 cm (12 inch) circle with a slightly raised edge. Brush the edge with the olive oil. Set aside.

Preheat the grill (broiler). Cook the capsicum, skin side up, until blistered and blackened all over. Remove from the heat and when cool enough to handle, remove and discard the skin and thinly slice the flesh.

Put the tomatoes in a saucepan and bring to the boil, then reduce the heat to low and simmer for 6–8 minutes, stirring occasionally, until most of the liquid has evaporated, leaving a fairly thick sauce; season to taste.

Spread the tomato sauce over the polenta base and top with the capsicum, tuna, ricotta and olives. Grill the pizza for 8–10 minutes, or until bubbling and golden brown. Sprinkle with the thyme leaves, cut into slices and serve hot.

Fibre fact

Polenta is a yellow granular flour made from corn (maize). It contains more fibre than rice or couscous, and here it is used to make a pizza base with much more fibre than the regular bread-type bases commonly available.

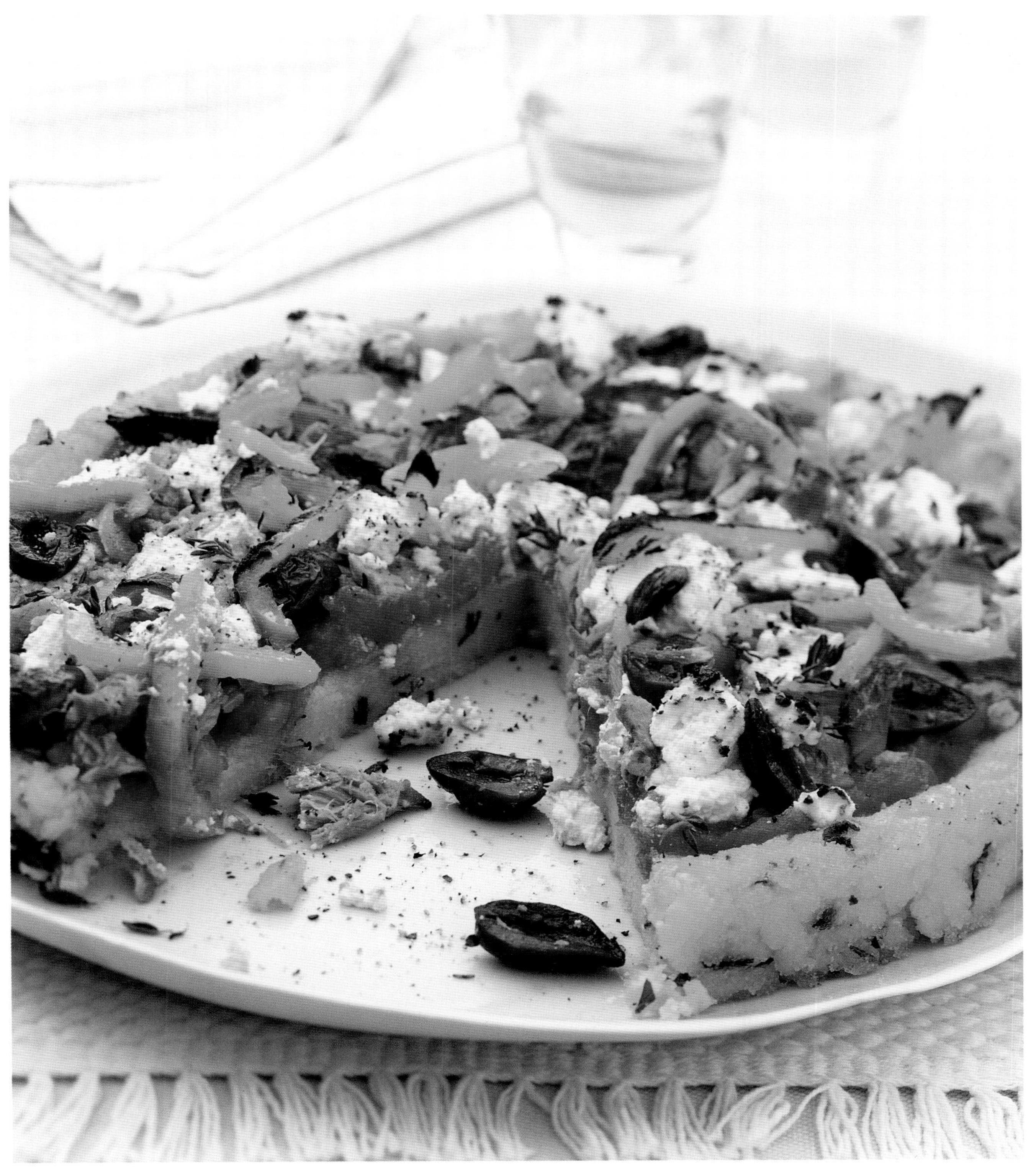

Focaccia with tomatoes & parsley

PREPARATION 25 minutes, plus 1 hour 40 minutes rising COOKING 40 minutes SERVES 8

Put the sugar into a large bowl with 2 cups (500 ml) lukewarm water and stir to combine. Sprinkle the yeast over the top, stir to dissolve and leave for 5 minutes, or until it starts to foam.

Reserve 2 tablespoons parsley for the top of the bread. Stir the remaining parsley into the yeast mixture with 1/4 cup (60 ml) of the olive oil, the sage and the salt, if using. Add 2 cups (300 g) of the flour and stir vigorously until well combined. Stir in the remaining flour to make a stiff dough.

Knead the dough on a lightly floured work surface for about 10 minutes, or until smooth and elastic. Place the dough in a lightly oiled bowl, turning to coat in the oil and cover loosely with plastic wrap. Leave in a warm draught-free place for about 1 hour, or until doubled in size.

Lightly oil a 43 x 28 cm (17 x 11 1/4 inch) swiss roll tin (jelly roll pan). Knock back the dough and knead briefly, then shape into a rectangle to fit the tin. Place in the tin, cover loosely with plastic wrap and set aside for 40 minutes, or until doubled in size.

Preheat the oven to 200°C (400°F/Gas 6). Make dimples in the top of the dough with your fingertips. Brush the remaining oil over the top and sprinkle with the garlic. Arrange the tomato and capsicum over the top and sprinkle with the parmesan. Bake on the lowest rack of the oven for 35–40 minutes, or until browned on the edges. Transfer to a wire rack to cool for at least 20 minutes. Sprinkle with the reserved parsley, cut into slices and serve.

Fibre fact

Puffy white focaccia is relatively low in fibre. In this recipe, wholemeal (whole-wheat) flour has been used to boost the fibre content of the base, while the topping of tomato and capsicum adds to the fibre and vitamins provided by this delicious Italian-style bread.

- 2 teaspoons sugar
- 2 teaspoons active dry (powdered) yeast
- 1/3 cup (10 g) chopped fresh flat-leaf parsley
- 1/3 cup (80 ml) olive oil
- 1/2 teaspoon dried sage
- 1 1/2 teaspoons salt (optional)
- 5 cups (750 g) wholemeal (whole-wheat) flour
- 2 cloves garlic, crushed
- 3 tomatoes, thinly sliced
- 1 large yellow capsicum (bell pepper), seeded and thinly sliced
- 2 tablespoons grated parmesan

Each serving provides
1564 kJ, 374 kcal, 12 g protein, 10 g fat (2 g saturated fat), 57 g carbohydrate (3 g sugars), 11 g fibre, 35 mg sodium

Spicy chicken tostadas

PREPARATION 25 minutes   COOKING 20 minutes   MAKES 8

500 g (1 lb) skinless, boneless chicken breasts
2 tablespoons extra virgin olive oil
2 red capsicums (bell peppers), seeded and chopped
1 onion, chopped
2 cloves garlic, thinly sliced
1 tablespoon mild chilli powder
2 teaspoons paprika
1 teaspoon ground cumin
410 g (15 oz) can chopped tomatoes
freshly ground black pepper
8 corn tortillas
410 g (15 oz) can borlotti or kidney beans
1 tomato, diced
pickled jalapeños (hot chillies) (optional)
1/2 iceberg lettuce, shredded
8 radishes, sliced
4 tablespoons low-fat sour cream or low-fat Greek-style yogurt, to serve
Tabasco sauce, to serve

Each serving (2 tostadas) provides
1976 kJ, 472 kcal, 37 g protein, 21 g fat (5 g saturated fat), 34 g carbohydrate (11 g sugars), 10 g fibre, 441 mg sodium

Place the chicken in a saucepan with enough cold water to cover. Bring to the boil, then reduce the heat to low and simmer for 10–15 minutes. Remove from the heat and leave to cool in the liquid. When cool enough to handle, drain and shred the meat. Set aside.

Meanwhile, heat the olive oil in a frying pan over medium heat. Add the capsicums, onion and garlic and cook for 5 minutes, or until the onion has softened. Add the chilli powder, paprika and cumin and cook for 3 minutes. Add the tomatoes and simmer for 5–8 minutes, or until thickened. Season, to taste, then remove from the heat and keep warm.

Heat a heavy-based frying pan over medium heat. Fry the tortillas, one at a time, for about 15 seconds on each side, or until slightly crisp and lightly browned. As they are done, stack them in a clean tea towel (dish cloth) to keep warm. Meanwhile, place the borlotti beans and their liquid in a small saucepan over medium heat and stir until warmed through. Drain well.

Place 2 toasted tortillas on each plate. Spread with the tomato mixture, then spoon over some beans and chicken. Add the diced tomato, pickled jalapeños, if using, lettuce and radishes. Finish with a spoonful of low-fat sour cream. Serve with Tabasco on the side for guests to help themselves.

Another idea

Instead of beans, you can use a mixture of 1 corn cob and 1 zucchini (courgette). Cook the corn and whole zucchini in a saucepan of boiling water until tender, about 10 minutes for the corn and 5 minutes for the zucchini. Drain well, then dice the zucchini and cut the corn kernels from the cob. Scatter the vegetables over the tortillas before adding the chicken.

Fibre fact

Pulses, such as borlotti and pinto beans, are a good source of soluble fibre and an excellent source of protein – and they are even better when they are eaten with grains such as wheat or maize (in corn tortillas).

Mexican bean burritos

PREPARATION 15 minutes   COOKING 10 minutes   SERVES 4 (makes 8)

- 8 soft flour tortillas
- 1 tablespoon vegetable oil
- 1 onion, chopped
- 2 cloves garlic, crushed
- 1 small green capsicum (bell pepper), seeded and chopped
- 1 small red capsicum (bell pepper), seeded and chopped
- 1 red chilli, seeded and finely chopped (optional)
- 1/2 teaspoon ground cumin
- 410 g (15 oz) can red kidney beans, rinsed and drained
- 1 cup (150 g) frozen corn kernels
- 1 large tomato, chopped
- 1/4 cup (60 g) salt-reduced tomato sauce (ketchup)
- 1 tablespoon hot chilli (pepper) sauce
- 2 tablespoons water
- 2 tablespoons chopped fresh coriander (cilantro) leaves
- 1/2 iceberg lettuce, shredded
- 1/2 cup (60 g) grated cheddar
- 1/2 cup (125 g) low-fat natural (plain) yogurt

Cook the tortillas following the packet instructions and keep warm in a low oven.

To make the filling, heat the vegetable oil in a large non-stick frying pan over medium heat. Add the onion, garlic and capsicums and cook for 5 minutes, or until the onion has softened. Add the chilli, if using, and the cumin, and stir for 1 minute until well combined.

Put the kidney beans onto a plate and lightly crush with a fork, then add to the frying pan with the corn and tomato. Stir in the tomato sauce, chilli sauce and 2 tablespoons water and continue to cook for a further 4 minutes. Stir in the coriander.

Serve the hot bean mixture, lettuce, cheese and yogurt in separate bowls for everyone to help themselves. To assemble a burrito, place some lettuce in the middle of a tortilla, spoon some of the bean mixture on top, add some grated cheese and top with a dollop of yogurt. Roll up and eat immediately.

Fibre fact

This recipe is very high in fibre thanks to the kidney beans, corn and other vegetables. You could increase the fibre content by using wholemeal (whole-wheat) tortillas.

Each serving (2 burritos) provides
1826 kJ, 436 kcal, 17 g protein, 15 g fat (6 g saturated fat), 55 g carbohydrate (13 g sugars), 10 g fibre, 402 mg sodium

Falafel pitas

PREPARATION 20 minutes, plus 30 minutes chilling   COOKING 15 minutes   SERVES 4

Falafels

2 x 410 g (15 oz) cans chickpeas, rinsed and drained

2 cloves garlic, crushed

1 teaspoon ground cumin

1 teaspoon ground coriander

1 green chilli, seeded and finely chopped

2 tablespoons chopped fresh coriander (cilantro) leaves

1 egg, lightly beaten

2 tablespoons wholemeal (whole-wheat) flour

freshly ground black pepper

2 tablespoons vegetable oil

To serve

1 1/3 cups (100 g) shredded red cabbage

1 carrot, grated

1 Lebanese (small) cucumber, cut into matchsticks

1 small red onion, thinly sliced

4 wholemeal (whole-wheat) pita breads

1/2 lemon, juiced

1/3 cup (75 g) low-fat hummus

Each serving provides
1951 kJ, 466 kcal, 19 g protein, 18 g fat (3 g saturated fat), 55 g carbohydrate (6 g sugars), 14 g fibre, 730 mg sodium

To make the falafels, put the chickpeas into a food processor or blender and process until smooth. Add the garlic, cumin and ground coriander and process again until well combined. Add the chilli, fresh coriander, egg and 1 tablespoon of the flour and process again briefly; season, to taste. Transfer to a bowl and refrigerate for about 30 minutes.

Lightly flour your hands with the remaining flour and shape the chickpea mixture into eight patties. Heat the vegetable oil in a frying pan and fry the patties, in batches, for about 3 minutes on each side, or until crisp and golden. Drain well on paper towel.

Meanwhile, to prepare the salad, put the cabbage, carrot, cucumber and onion in a bowl and mix well to combine. Set aside. Heat the pita breads in a toaster or under a hot grill (broiler). Stir the lemon juice into the hummus to thin it slightly.

To serve, cut a slit lengthwise in the side of each pita to form a pocket. Spread 1 tablespoon of hummus inside each pocket, then stuff in two falafels with some salad. Serve immediately.

Fibre fact

The falafel contains chickpeas and the hummus is a dip or spread made of blended chickpeas. Chickpeas are high in protein and fibre but low in fat.

Vegetarian pilaf

PREPARATION 15 minutes   COOKING 25 minutes   SERVES 4

1 teaspoon canola oil
1 large onion, finely chopped
2 large cloves garlic, crushed
$1^1/_2$ teaspoons ground coriander
1 teaspoon ground cinnamon
1 teaspoon turmeric
1 pinch of crushed dried chillies (optional)
410 g (15 oz) can butterbeans (lima beans) or chickpeas, rinsed and drained
$^1/_2$ cup (90 g) dried apricots, chopped
$1^1/_4$ cup (220 g) burghul (bulgur)
150 g (5 oz) green beans, halved
freshly ground black pepper
2 hard-boiled eggs, peeled and sliced
fresh coriander (cilantro) leaves, to serve

Each serving provides
1753 kJ, 419 kcal, 19 g protein, 6 g fat (1 g saturated fat), 70 g carbohydrate (15 g sugars), 21 g fibre, 207 mg sodium

Heat the canola oil in a large saucepan over medium–high heat. Add the onion and garlic and cook for 5 minutes, or until the onion softens. Stir in the ground coriander, cinnamon, turmeric and chillies (if using). Add the butterbeans and apricots, and stir to coat them with the spices.

Add the burghul and green beans to the pan, stirring to coat in the spices, then pour in enough water to cover by about 1 cm ($^1/_2$ inch). Bring to the boil, then reduce the heat to low, cover and simmer for 20 minutes, or until all of the liquid has been absorbed and the burghul is tender. Remove from the heat and use a fork to fluff the grains; season, to taste.

Serve the pilaf hot, garnished with the egg slices and sprinkled with coriander leaves.

Fibre fact

Apricots are a useful source of fibre. Keep a packet of ready-to-eat dried apricots handy for a quick snack.

Chickpea & pita salad

PREPARATION 15 minutes   COOKING 5 minutes   SERVES 5

3 wholemeal (whole-wheat) pita breads
2 x 410 g (15 oz) cans chickpeas, rinsed and drained
1/2 telegraph (long) cucumber, chopped
4 large tomatoes, chopped
6 spring onions (scallions), chopped
1/2 cup (80 g) pitted kalamata olives
sprigs of fresh mint, to garnish

Dressing

2 tablespoons extra virgin olive oil
1 tablespoon balsamic vinegar
2 tablespoons olive tapenade
1 tablespoon chopped fresh mint
freshly ground black pepper

Preheat the grill (broiler). Split the pita breads in half and open with a sharp knife. Toast under the grill for 5 minutes, or until golden brown and crisp, turning once, then leave to cool. Tear into bite-sized pieces.

Put the chickpeas, cucumber, tomatoes, spring onions and olives in a serving bowl.

To make the dressing, whisk together the olive oil, vinegar, tapenade, mint and season, to taste. Drizzle the dressing over the chickpea mixture then toss together until well combined.

Just before serving, add the pieces of pita bread and mix well. Serve garnished with sprigs of fresh mint.

Fibre fact

Olives are the base ingredient of tapenade. It consists of puréed or finely chopped olives in olive oil, plus other ingredients such as capers, anchovies or garlic. Olives are a great source of fibre. 100 g (3 1/2 oz) of olives contain 3 g fibre.

Each serving provides
1660 kJ, 395 kcal, 15 g protein, 16 g fat (2 g saturated fat), 47 g carbohydrate (8 g sugars), 11 g fibre, 776 mg sodium

Stir-fried vegetable curry

PREPARATION 25 minutes, plus overnight soaking   COOKING 1 hour   SERVES 4

Blanch the pickling onions in a saucepan of boiling water for 3 minutes. Drain well and peel when cool enough to handle. Set aside.

Meanwhile, add the mung beans to the pan of boiling water and boil rapidly for 10 minutes, then reduce the heat and simmer for 20–25 minutes, or until tender. Drain well and set aside.

Bring the stock to the boil in a separate saucepan, add the coconut cream and stir well to combine. Set aside.

Using a pestle and mortar, pound the ginger and garlic to a paste. Stir in the ground coriander, garam masala, turmeric and dried chillies until well blended.

Heat 2 tablespoons of the canola oil in a large wok over high heat. Add the coriander, cumin and mustard seeds and cook for 30 seconds, or until the seeds become aromatic. Use a slotted spoon to remove the seeds to a plate lined with paper towel. Add the remaining oil and the spice paste to the wok. Reduce the heat to medium and stir-fry for 1 minute. Stir in the carrots, parsnips, potatoes and 2 tablespoons water; stir-fry for a further 2 minutes.

Add the coconut stock to the wok and bring to the boil, then reduce the heat to low, cover, and simmer for 5 minutes. Add the cauliflower, peas and onions. Cover and simmer for a further 5 minutes, stirring occasionally. Uncover and bring back to the boil, then boil for about 5 minutes, or until most of the liquid has evaporated and all of the vegetables are just tender.

Add the cabbage, mung beans and fried spice seeds to the curry and stir-fry until the cabbage has wilted. Season, to taste, and serve immediately, sprinkled with coriander, if using.

Fibre fact

Serve with brown rice for extra fibre benefits.

- 125 g (4 oz) small pickling onions (unpeeled)
- 125 g (4 oz) dried mung beans, soaked overnight, rinsed and drained
- 1 3/4 cups (435 ml) salt-reduced vegetable stock
- 1/4 cup (60 ml) low-fat coconut cream
- 1 tablespoon grated fresh ginger
- 1 clove garlic, crushed
- 1 1/2 tablespoons ground coriander
- 1 tablespoon garam masala
- 1/2 teaspoon turmeric
- 1/8 teaspoon crushed dried chillies
- 1/4 cup (60 ml) canola oil
- 1 teaspoon coriander seeds, crushed
- 1 teaspoon cumin seeds
- 1 teaspoon brown mustard seeds
- 250 g (8 oz) carrots, diced
- 250 g (8 oz) parsnips, diced
- 250 g (8 oz) small new potatoes, halved
- 250 g (8 oz) cauliflower, cut into small florets
- 150 g (5 oz) frozen peas
- 2 cups (150 g) shredded white cabbage
- freshly ground black pepper
- chopped fresh coriander (cilantro) leaves, to garnish (optional)

Each serving provides
1785 kJ, 422 kcal, 17 g protein, 18 g fat (4 g saturated fat), 49 g carbohydrate (14 g sugars), 9 g fibre, 521 mg sodium

Thai-style beef sandwich with coleslaw

PREPARATION 10 minutes, plus 30 minutes marinating   COOKING 10 minutes   SERVES 4

- 2 tablespoons tomato paste (concentrated purée)
- 1/2 cup (125 ml) lime juice
- 1 1/2 teaspoons ground coriander
- 500 g (1 lb) sirloin steak, eye fillet or flank steak, trimmed of fat
- 1 teaspoon sugar (optional)
- 1 teaspoon dried red chilli flakes
- 3 cups (225 g) shredded green cabbage
- 2 carrots, coarsely grated
- 1 large red capsicum (bell pepper), seeded and cut into matchsticks
- 1/2 cup (15 g) chopped fresh coriander (cilantro) leaves
- 1/3 cup (10 g) chopped fresh mint
- 4 wholemeal (whole-wheat) bread rolls, halved

Each serving provides
1706 kJ, 408 kcal, 35 g protein, 11 g fat (4 g saturated fat), 43 g carbohydrate (8 g sugars), 8 g fibre, 564 mg sodium

Mix the tomato paste in a bowl with half of the lime juice and the ground coriander. Add the steak, turning to coat, then cover with plastic wrap and refrigerate for 30 minutes.

To make the coleslaw, whisk the remaining lime juice in a large bowl with the sugar, if using, and chilli flakes. Add the cabbage, carrots, capsicum, coriander and mint and toss thoroughly to combine. Refrigerate until ready to serve.

Preheat a chargrill pan or barbecue hotplate to high. Remove the steak from the marinade and cook for 4 minutes on each side for medium–rare, brushing any remaining marinade over the steak halfway through cooking. Let stand for 10 minutes. Cut the steak on the diagonal, across the grain, into thin slices.

To serve, fill each bread roll with a little of the coleslaw and top with some steak slices. Serve any leftover coleslaw on the side.

Fibre fact

Cabbage is packed with anti-oxidants and it is naturally high in fibre. Choose wholemeal (whole-wheat) rolls for extra fibre.

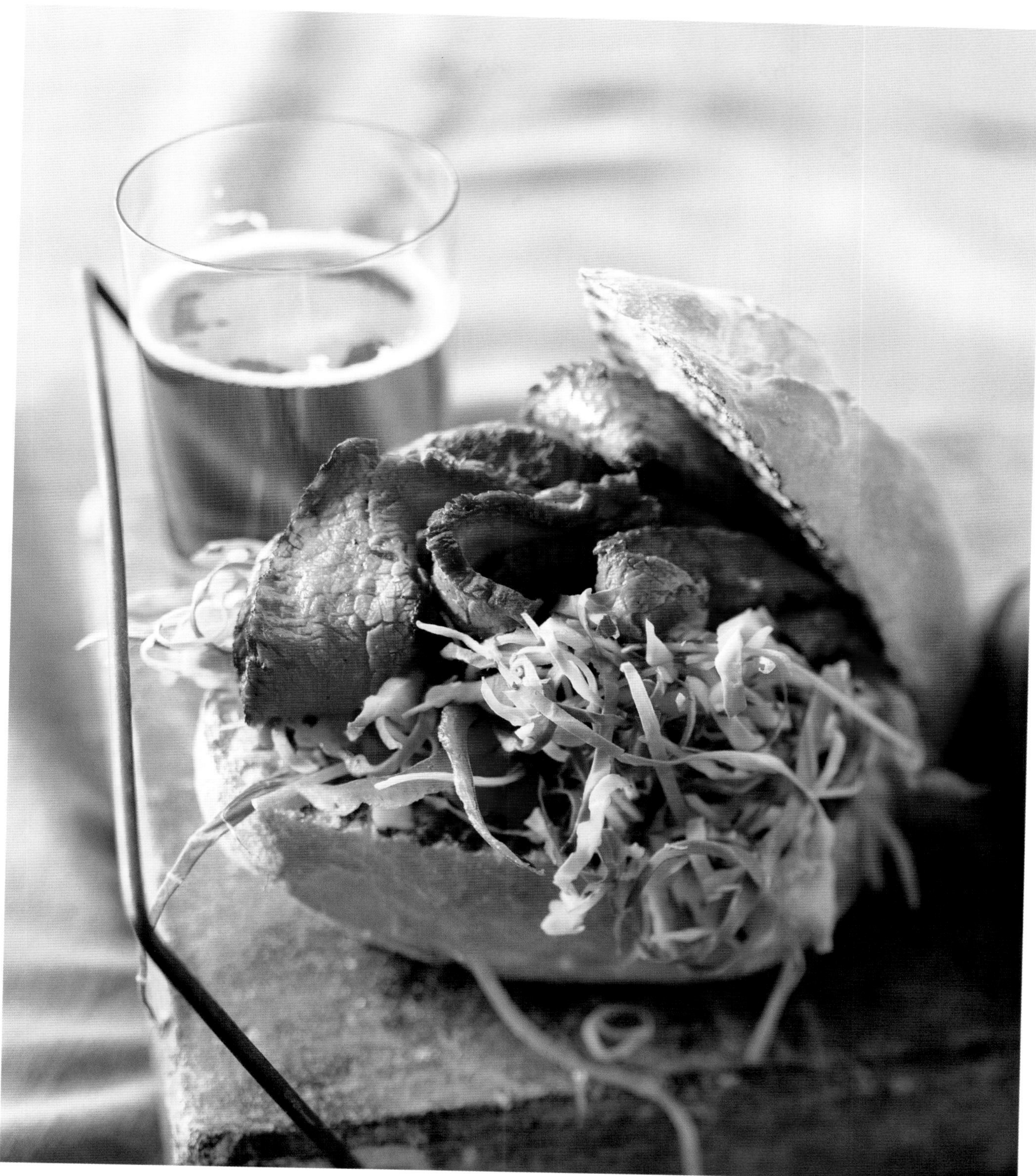

Vegetable burgers

PREPARATION 20 minutes   COOKING 25 minutes   SERVES 4

Heat 2 tablespoons of the olive oil in a large non-stick frying pan over medium heat. Add the onion and garlic and cook for 5 minutes, or until the onion has softened. Add the carrots and zucchini and cook for a further 10 minutes, stirring frequently, until the vegetables soften. Stir in the cumin and ground coriander, peanut butter and fresh coriander. Season, to taste, then mix well to combine. Remove the pan from the heat and set aside to cool slightly.

Add the breadcrumbs and egg to the vegetable mixture and mix well to combine. Shape into 4 thick patties, about 10 cm (4 inches) in diameter.

Heat the remaining oil in a clean frying pan over medium–low heat. Cook the patties for 5 minutes on each side, or until they are firm and golden.

To serve, stir together the tomatoes, tomato sauce and a little pepper in a bowl. Split the hamburger buns in half and toast the cut sides. Spread 1/2 teaspoon mayonnaise on each piece of bun, then place some lettuce and a patty on top of half of the buns. Spread with the tomato mixture and top with the shallot slices. Replace the tops of the buns and serve.

Fibre fact

Peanut butter contributes protein and fibre to these burgers, as does the wheat from the wholemeal (whole-wheat) breadcrumbs. Peanut butter is high in fat, but this is largely in a healthy monounsaturated form. Use a good-quality crunchy or whole nut natural peanut butter and for extra fibre, use wholemeal (whole-wheat) buns.

2 1/2 tablespoons extra virgin olive oil
1 large onion, finely chopped
1 clove garlic, finely chopped
300 g (10 oz) carrots, coarsely grated
300 g (10 oz) zucchini (courgettes), coarsely grated
1 1/2 teaspoons ground cumin
1 1/2 teaspoons ground coriander
1/4 cup (60 g) natural peanut butter
2 tablespoons chopped fresh coriander (cilantro) leaves
freshly ground black pepper
1 1/3 cups (105 g) fresh wholemeal (whole-wheat) breadcrumbs
1 egg, lightly beaten

To serve

2 tomatoes, seeded and chopped
2 tablespoons tomato sauce (ketchup), chutney or relish
4 sesame burger buns
1 tablespoon low-fat mayonnaise
4 iceberg lettuce leaves, shredded
1 French shallot (eschalot), thinly sliced

Each serving provides
2542 kJ, 607 kcal, 19 g protein, 26 g fat (4 g saturated fat), 75 g carbohydrate (18 g sugars), 10 g fibre, 851 mg sodium

Main Dishes

New England simmered beef

PREPARATION 25 minutes COOKING 1½ hours SERVES 4

500 g (1 lb) piece of stewing beef (such as chuck, brisket or blade steak)

3 sprigs of fresh thyme

3 sprigs of fresh flat-leaf parsley

1 bay leaf

2 cloves garlic, sliced

10 black peppercorns, lightly crushed

250 g (8 oz) leek, white part only, sliced

1 celery stalk, sliced

300 g (10 oz) baby new potatoes, scrubbed

12 French shallots (eschalots)

300 g (10 oz) baby turnips, trimmed

300 g (10 oz) baby carrots, trimmed

150 g (5 oz) savoy cabbage, thinly sliced

finely chopped fresh parsley, to serve

Beetroot and onion relish

350 g (12 oz) cooked beetroot (beets), peeled and cubed

6 spring onions (scallions), finely chopped

2 tablespoons finely chopped fresh flat-leaf parsley

Each serving provides
1580 kJ, 377 kcal, 45 g protein, 8 g fat (3 g saturated fat), 32 g carbohydrate (19 g sugars), 12 g fibre, 241 mg sodium

Put the beef in a large flameproof casserole dish over high heat. Add enough water to cover the meat and bring to the boil, skimming the surface as necessary to remove any impurities. Tie the thyme, parsley, bay leaf, garlic and peppercorns securely in a little cheesecloth (muslin) bag and add to the pan with the leek and celery. Reduce the heat to low, partially cover the dish, and simmer gently, skimming the surface to remove any impurities, for 1–1½ hours, or until the beef is very tender.

To make the beetroot relish, combine the beetroot in a bowl with the spring onions and parsley. Cover and refrigerate until ready to serve.

Preheat the oven to 135°C (275°F/Gas 1). When the meat is tender, transfer it to a smaller ovenproof dish and spoon over enough of the cooking liquid to cover the meat. Cover with foil and place in the oven to keep warm until ready to serve.

Remove the herbs from the casserole dish and discard. Add the potatoes and shallots to the dish, increase the heat to medium and cook for 5 minutes. Add the turnips and carrots and simmer for a further 15 minutes, or until all the vegetables are tender. Using a slotted spoon, transfer all the vegetables to the dish with the meat.

Add the cabbage to the broth in the casserole dish and simmer for about 3 minutes, or until tender. Remove from the dish with a slotted spoon and add to the other vegetables.

To serve, slice the beef against the grain and place the slices in shallow bowls. Top with a selection of vegetables and spoon over some of the broth. Sprinkle with parsley and serve with a dollop of the beetroot relish on top.

Fibre fact

Different countries have different food guidelines, but health authorities agree that a daily intake of at least five serves of vegetables is recommended to ensure adequate vitamins, minerals and fibre. Each serve of this delicious recipe provides your daily five serves of vegetables as well as oxidant-rich herbs and spices.

Beef & chickpea tagine

PREPARATION 10 minutes COOKING 4 hours SERVES 4

- 300 g (10 oz) stewing beef (such as chuck, brisket or blade steak)
- 1/2 teaspoon ground nutmeg
- 1/2 teaspoon ground cardamom
- 1/2 teaspoon ground allspice
- 1 tablespoon ground cumin
- 1 tablespoon ground cinnamon
- 2 teaspoons ground ginger
- 1 tablespoon paprika
- 1 pinch of ground cloves
- 1 tablespoon olive oil
- 1 large onion, diced
- 1 small bunch of coriander (cilantro), leaves picked, stalks finely chopped
- 1 large carrot, diced
- 1 2/3 cups (420 ml) salt-reduced vegetable stock or water
- 400 g (14 oz) can chickpeas, rinsed and drained
- 410 g (15 oz) can chopped tomatoes
- 1 small zucchini (courgette), diced
- 1 small red or yellow capsicum (bell pepper), seeded and diced
- 1/4 cup (50 g) pitted prunes
- 1/4 cup (50 g) pitted dates
- 1/3 cup (50 g) pitted olives, halved
- 1/2 preserved lemon, flesh discarded, peel rinsed and thinly sliced
- 2 tablespoons flaked almonds, lightly toasted

Cut the beef into 2 cm (3/4 inch) chunks and place in a glass dish. Combine the spices and add to the dish, tossing to evenly coat the beef. Set aside.

Preheat the oven to 120°C (250°F/Gas 1/4–1/2). Heat the olive oil in a flameproof casserole dish with a tight-fitting lid. Add the onion and coriander stalks and cook over medium heat for about 5 minutes, or until the onion softens. Add the carrot and cook for a further 2 minutes, then add the beef and continue cooking for 5 minutes, turning regularly, until the beef is brown on all sides.

Add the stock to the dish and stir well to lift up any bits stuck to the base. Add the chickpeas and tomatoes and stir well to combine. Cover with the lid and transfer to the oven to cook for 2 hours.

Remove the dish from the oven, add the zucchini, capsicum, prunes, dates, olives and preserved lemon and stir well to combine. Return to the oven to cook for a further 1 hour. Remove the lid and bake for an additional 1 hour, or until the beef is very soft and falling apart – you may need to check the dish every now and then and top up with a little water as needed. Scatter the flaked almonds and coriander leaves over the top and serve the tagine with couscous on the side.

Each serving provides:
1636 kJ, 391 kcal, 25 g protein, 16 g fat (3 g saturated fat), 40 g carbohydrate (22 g sugars), 11 g fibre, 1093 mg sodium

Fibre fact

Tagines traditionally contain fruit, nuts and legumes along with the meat, fantastic sources of extra fibre and flavour. You can use other nuts such as pistachio or cashew nuts, and other fruits that work well are dried currants, dried apricots and dried peaches, or try adding fresh diced apple or poached quince.

Chilli con carne with cornbread

PREPARATION 20 minutes   COOKING 1½ hours   SERVES 6

- 1 tablespoon extra virgin olive oil
- 350 g (12 oz) lean stewing beef (such as chuck, brisket or blade steak), cut into 2 cm (3/4 inch) chunks
- 1 large onion, diced
- 2 cloves garlic, crushed
- 1/2 teaspoon cumin seeds
- 1 teaspoon dried red chilli flakes
- 1 tablespoon tomato paste (concentrated purée)
- 410 g (15 oz) can chopped tomatoes
- 2 x 400 g (14 oz) cans red kidney beans, rinsed and drained
- 300 ml (10 fl oz) salt-reduced beef stock

Cornbread

- 1 cup (125 g) fine polenta (cornmeal)
- 1 cup (150 g) plain (all-purpose) flour
- 2 teaspoons baking powder
- 1 egg
- 1 cup (250 ml) low-fat milk
- 1 cup (150 g/about 1 corn cob) fresh or frozen corn kernels, thawed if frozen
- 1 small fresh green chilli, seeded and finely chopped

Each serving provides
1794 kJ, 420 kcal, 28 g protein, 9 g fat (2 g saturated fat), 55 g carbohydrate (10 g sugars), 9 g fibre, 597 mg sodium

To make the chilli con carne, heat the olive oil in a large heavy-based saucepan over high heat. Add the beef and cook for 3–4 minutes, stirring regularly, until brown on all sides. Remove to a plate.

Reduce the heat to low, add the onion to the pan and cook gently for 8–10 minutes, or until the onion starts to colour. Add the garlic, cumin seeds and chilli flakes and cook for 1 minute, stirring well to coat the onion. Return the meat to the pan and add the tomato paste, tomatoes, kidney beans and stock. Stir well and bring to the boil, then reduce the heat to low, cover, and simmer for 1–1 1/2 hours, or until the meat is tender.

Meanwhile, make the cornbread. Preheat the oven to 200°C (400°F/Gas 6) and lightly grease a shallow 20 cm (8 inch) square cake tin. Put the polenta, flour and baking powder into a mixing bowl and stir well to combine. In a separate bowl, combine the egg and milk, then add to the flour mixture, stirring until just combined – do not overmix or the bread will be tough. Lightly fold in the corn and chilli to combine. Spoon the mixture into the prepared tin and bake for 20–25 minutes, or until firm to the touch. Allow to cool in the tin for 10 minutes, before turning out and cutting into slices.

Serve the chilli con carne in warmed bowls with chunks of the warm cornbread on the side.

Fibre fact

Kidney beans are a hearty high-fibre addition to this beef chilli. Combining legumes and meat has many health benefits; for example, the iron in legumes is more easily absorbed by your body when you eat them in a dish containing meat. To increase your fibre intake even further, serve this dish with plenty of green salad or vegetables on the side.

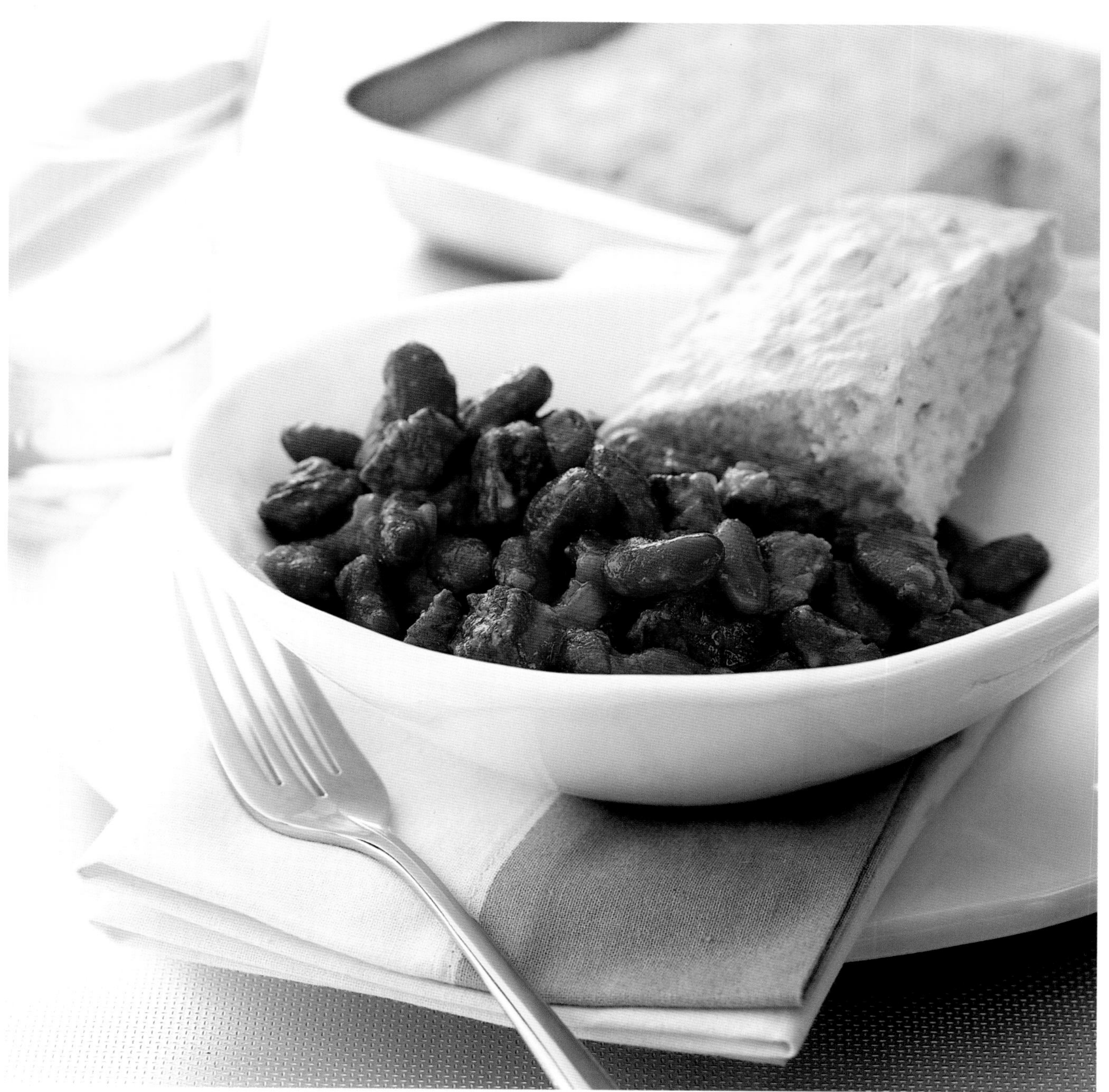

Mediterranean lamb stew

PREPARATION 20 minutes   COOKING 2¾ hours   SERVES 6

Heat 1 tablespoon of the olive oil in a flameproof casserole dish over medium heat. Add the onions and garlic and cook for 8–10 minutes, or until golden. Remove to a plate.

Heat the remaining oil in the casserole dish over medium–high heat. Add the lamb and cook for about 3 minutes, turning to brown evenly on all sides. Sprinkle the flour and rosemary over the lamb and cook for a further 1½ minutes, or until all of the flour is absorbed.

Return the onions to the dish with 1 cup (250 ml) of the stock and the tomato juice. Bring to the boil, cover, then reduce the heat to low and simmer for 1 hour. Stir in the chickpeas, cover, and continue cooking for a further 1–1¼ hours, or until the lamb is almost tender.

Stir in the zucchini, tomatoes, pepper and basil, adding more stock if the stew is becoming too thick, and cook for about 15 minutes, or until the lamb is very tender when pierced with a fork. Divide among serving bowls and serve immediately.

Fibre fact

The fibre in this dish comes from the chickpeas and vegetables. You can increase the proportion of these (and decrease the meat) to increase the fibre content. Serve with wholegrain bread on the side to boost your fibre intake even further.

1½ tablespoons olive oil

2 large onions, sliced

2 cloves garlic, finely chopped

750 g (1½ lb) boned lean lamb shoulder, trimmed and cut into 2.5 cm (1 inch) cubes

1 tablespoon plain (all-purpose) flour

2 teaspoons chopped fresh rosemary, or 1 teaspoon dried rosemary

1–1¾ cups (250–435 ml) salt-reduced beef stock

350 ml (12 fl oz) tomato juice

410 g (15 oz) can chickpeas, rinsed and drained

2 zucchini (courgettes), diced

350 g (12 oz) cherry tomatoes, halved

1 pinch freshly ground black pepper

2 teaspoons chopped fresh basil or 1 teaspoon dried basil

Each serving provides
1197 kJ, 286 kcal, 28 g protein, 12 g fat (4 g saturated fat), 16 g carbohydrate (7 g sugars), 5 g fibre, 697 mg sodium

Persian-style lamb shanks with figs

PREPARATION 30 minutes COOKING 2 hours SERVES 4

- 2 x 350 g (12 oz) lamb shanks
- 2 tablespoons olive oil
- 6 French shallots (eschalots), quartered
- 3 cloves garlic, chopped
- 2 sprigs fresh rosemary
- 1 bay leaf
- 500 g (1 lb) tomatoes, peeled and quartered
- 1 1/2 cups (300 g) green lentils
- 2 tablespoons pomegranate molasses
- 1 tablespoon honey
- 3 cups (750 ml) salt-reduced lamb, beef or vegetable stock
- 8 dried figs, quartered
- 2 zucchini (courgettes), thickly sliced
- 2 tablespoons chopped fresh coriander (cilantro) leaves

Each serving provides
2865 kJ, 685 kcal, 49 g protein, 22 g fat (7 g saturated fat), 74 g carbohydrate (35 g sugars), 19 g fibre, 576 mg sodium

Preheat the oven to 220°C (425°F/Gas 7). Put the lamb shanks in a large flameproof casserole dish and roast in the oven for 25 minutes, or until they are a rich brown colour on the outside. Remove the shanks from the dish and drain on paper towel. Reduce the oven temperature to 160°C (320°F/Gas 2–3).

Heat the olive oil in the casserole dish over medium heat. Add the shallots and cook for 5 minutes, stirring until lightly browned. Stir in the garlic, rosemary, bay leaf and tomatoes and cook for 1 minute. Stir in the lentils, then return the lamb shanks to the dish, pushing them down into the vegetable mixture.

Stir the pomegranate molasses and honey into the stock with 1/3 cup (80 ml) water, then add to the dish. Slowly bring to the boil, then cover the casserole dish with a tight-fitting lid and cook for 45 minutes.

Remove the casserole from the oven, add a little more stock if the mixture is too dry, then stir in the figs and zucchini (this is easier if you lift out the lamb shanks first, then return them after stirring). Cover and bake for a further 45 minutes, or until the lamb is very tender. Lift out the lamb and carve the meat from the shanks. Discard the bones and return the meat to the casserole. Gently stir, then serve scattered with coriander.

Fibre fact

For centuries figs have been prized for their sweetness and easy preservation by drying. Thanks to their seeds and skin, figs are one of the highest-fibre fruits, and in this recipe they add to the high fibre content along with lentils and zucchini.

Pork & bean chilli

PREPARATION 20 minutes COOKING 2 hours SERVES 4

750 g ($1^1/_2$ lb) pork shoulder, cut into 1 cm ($^1/_2$ inch) cubes

$^1/_2$ cup (70 g) plain (all-purpose) flour

$^1/_4$ cup (60 ml) olive oil

1 large onion, finely chopped

1 green capsicum (bell pepper), seeded and chopped

1 jalapeño (hot chilli), seeded and finely chopped

3 cloves garlic, crushed

2 x 410 g (15 oz) cans chopped tomatoes

1 cup (250 ml) salt-reduced chicken stock

3 tablespoons chilli powder

2 x 410 g (15 oz) cans butterbeans (lima beans) or cannellini beans, rinsed and drained

fresh coriander (cilantro) leaves, to garnish

Put the pork in a bowl with the flour and toss well to coat, shaking off any excess. Heat 1 tablespoon of the olive oil in a large non-stick saucepan over medium–high heat. Cook half of the pork for about 5 minutes, turning regularly until brown on all sides. Remove to a plate. Heat another 1 tablespoon of the oil and cook the remaining pork, then remove to the plate.

Heat the remaining oil in the pan over medium heat. Add the onion, capsicum, chilli and garlic and cook for 5 minutes, or until the onion has softened. Return the pork to pan, then add the tomatoes, stock and chilli powder and simmer for about 1 hour, stirring occasionally.

Stir in the beans and continue to simmer for about 40 minutes, or until the meat is tender and the sauce has thickened. Divide among serving bowls and garnish with coriander to serve.

Fibre fact

To increase the fibre content of this dish, decrease the amount of meat and increase the beans. Serve with steamed brown rice or cornbread for even more fibre.

Each serving provides
1645 kJ, 393 kcal, 34 g protein, 16 g fat (3 g saturated fat), 24 g carbohydrate (8 g sugars), 9 g fibre, 448 mg sodium

Pork & plum stir-fry

PREPARATION 10 minutes COOKING 10 minutes SERVES 4

300 g (10 oz) pork leg steak
1/3 cup (80 ml) shaoxing rice wine
1/4 cup (60 ml) canola oil
1 teaspoon sugar
1 tablespoon Chinese five-spice
2 cloves garlic, crushed
2 cm (3/4 inch) piece of ginger, peeled and thinly sliced
1/2 cup (100 g) fresh or canned baby corn
50 g (1 3/4 oz) snow peas (mangetout), trimmed
1 large celery stalk, thinly sliced
150 g (5 oz) Chinese broccoli (gai larn) or baby bok choy, chopped
50 g (1 3/4 oz) oyster mushrooms, stalks removed
50 g (1 3/4 oz) mung bean sprouts
2 large plums, stones removed and cut into thin wedges
2 spring onions (scallions), cut into 2 cm (3/4 inch) lengths
1 tablespoon dark salt-reduced soy sauce
2 teaspoons cornflour (cornstarch)

Each serving provides:
1164 kJ, 278 kcal, 18 g protein, 16 g fat (2 g saturated fat), 11 g carbohydrate (6 g sugars), 4 g fibre, 244 mg sodium

Cut the pork into thin strips and place in a glass dish. Add 1/4 cup (60 ml) of the shaoxing rice wine and 1 tablespoon of the canola oil, then sprinkle with the sugar, Chinese five-spice and toss well to evenly coat the pork. Set aside to marinate.

Heat 1 tablespoon of the canola oil in a wok or large heavy-based saucepan over high heat. Add the pork and cook for about 2 minutes, turning once, until just starting to brown. Remove to a plate. Wipe the wok clean with paper towel.

Heat the remaining canola oil in the clean wok over high heat. Add the garlic and ginger and stir-fry briefly, then add the fresh baby corn, if using, and stir-fry for 1 minute. Add the snow peas and celery and stir-fry for 1 minute, then add the Chinese broccoli and stir-fry for a further 1 minute. Add the oyster mushrooms, mung bean sprouts, baby corn (if canned) and plums and stir gently until the mushrooms are just cooked. Return the pork to the wok with the spring onions and stir to combine and heat through.

Combine the soy sauce, remaining shaoxing rice wine and the cornflour in a small bowl, then add to the side of the wok, stirring gently to combine. Serve immediately with steamed rice on the side.

Fibre fact

This stir-fry is based on a Chinese recipe. Instead of the traditional plum sauce, fresh plums are used for added fibre and tang. To increase the fibre even further, serve with steamed brown rice. Brown rice has three times the fibre of white; it does take longer to cook, but this doesn't have to be a problem: simply start cooking your rice before you begin this recipe and it will be ready at the same time.

Mediterranean chicken

PREPARATION 20 minutes COOKING 1 hour SERVES 4

Preheat the oven to 180°C (350°F/Gas 4). Heat the olive oil in a flameproof casserole dish with a tight-fitting lid, over medium–high heat. Dust the chicken pieces in the flour to coat, then cook for about 4 minutes on each side or until just golden. Remove to a plate.

Add the fennel to the pan, reduce the heat to medium and cook for 7 minutes, stirring frequently, until the fennel is golden. Add the garlic and cook for 1 minute, then add the stock, lemon juice, rosemary and thyme. Bring to the boil, then add the chicken, cover the dish and transfer to the oven to cook for 35 minutes, or until the chicken is cooked through.

Just before you are ready to serve, stir in the cannellini and green beans and cook for a further 5 minutes, or until the beans are tender and heated through. Remove from the heat, divide among serving bowls and serve immediately.

Fibre fact

Green and dried beans provide different types of fibre so they are a great combination in this dish, complemented with high-fibre fennel. To increase the fibre further, serve with salad and wholegrain bread on the side.

2 tablespoons olive oil

1.75 kg (3 1/2 lb) whole chicken, cut into 8 portions, skin removed

1/4 cup (35 g) plain (all-purpose) flour

1 large fennel bulb, trimmed and sliced

4 cloves garlic, thinly sliced

1 cup (250 ml) salt-reduced chicken stock

2 tablespoons lemon juice

1/4 teaspoon dried rosemary

1/4 teaspoon thyme

2 x 300 g (10 oz) cans cannellini or butterbeans (lima beans), rinsed and drained

250 g (8 oz) green beans, cut into 5 cm (2 inch) lengths

Each serving provides
2418 kJ, 578 kcal, 51 g protein, 27 g fat (7 g saturated fat), 29 g carbohydrate (10 g sugars), 14 g fibre, 617 mg sodium

Aromatic chicken with couscous

PREPARATION 20 minutes   COOKING 20 minutes   SERVES 4

1 tablespoon olive oil

4 skinless, boneless chicken breasts, cut into 1 cm (1/2 inch) thick strips

1 large onion, finely chopped

2 cloves garlic, finely chopped

1 teaspoon ground cumin

1 teaspoon ground coriander

1 cinnamon stick

2 large zucchini (courgettes), halved lengthwise and sliced

410 g (15 oz) can chopped tomatoes

200 ml (7 fl oz) salt-reduced vegetable stock

250 g (8 oz) sugar snap peas

410 g (15 oz) can chickpeas, rinsed and drained

Couscous

1 1/4 cups (230 g) instant couscous

400 ml (14 fl oz) boiling water

1 tablespoon olive oil

1/2 tablespoon butter

freshly ground black pepper

chopped fresh coriander (cilantro) leaves, to serve

Each serving provides
2568 kJ, 613 kcal, 43 g protein, 20 g fat (5 g saturated fat), 65 g carbohydrate (9 g sugars), 9 g fibre, 543 mg sodium

Heat the olive oil in a wok or heavy-based frying pan over medium–high heat. Add the chicken, onion and garlic and cook for about 2 minutes, stirring constantly until the chicken is sealed on all sides. Reduce the heat to low, add the cumin, coriander and cinnamon and cook, stirring constantly, for 1 minute. Add the zucchini and stir well, then add the tomatoes and stock and cook for 5 minutes, stirring occasionally. Add the sugar snap peas and chickpeas and cook for a further 5 minutes, stirring frequently.

To make the couscous, put it in a baking dish (off the heat) and pour over the boiling water. Add the olive oil, stir well, then cover and leave to soak for 5 minutes. Add the butter and stir well to combine, then place over medium heat for 3 minutes. Remove from the heat and fluff up the grains with a fork to separate them; season, to taste.

To serve, pile the couscous onto serving plates and spoon the chicken over the top, garnishing with fresh coriander.

Fibre fact

Chickpeas have been cultivated since neolithic times, and are recognised as highly nutritious and easy to store. Like other members of the legume family, they add significant soluble and insoluble fibre to any dish.

Curried chicken & vegetables

PREPARATION 15 minutes   COOKING 35 minutes   SERVES 4

- 1 tablespoon turmeric
- $1^1/_2$ teaspoons ground ginger
- $^1/_2$ teaspoon ground cinnamon
- $^1/_2$ teaspoon sugar
- $^1/_2$ teaspoon freshly ground black pepper
- 600 g ($1^1/_4$ lb) skinless, boneless chicken thighs, cut into 2.5 cm (1 inch) pieces
- 2 teaspoons olive oil
- 1 onion, thickly sliced
- 4 cloves garlic, crushed
- 3 carrots, thickly sliced
- 500 g (1 lb) small red-skinned potatoes, quartered
- 2 teaspoons smooth peanut butter
- 4 cups (250 g) small broccoli florets

In a medium bowl, stir together the turmeric, ginger, cinnamon, sugar and pepper. Add the chicken pieces, tossing well to evenly coat in the spices.

Heat the olive oil in a flameproof casserole dish over medium heat. Add the onion and garlic and cook for 5 minutes, stirring frequently, or until the onion softens.

Add the carrots, potatoes and peanut butter to the dish with $^1/_2$ cup (125 ml) water. Bring to the boil, then reduce the heat to medium and simmer for 5 minutes, or until the carrots begin to soften.

Add the chicken to the dish and cook for 2 minutes, or until it is no longer pink. Stir in 2 cups (500 ml) water. Bring back to the boil, then reduce the heat to low, cover and simmer for 15 minutes, or until the chicken is cooked through and the potatoes are tender. Just before you are ready to serve, add the broccoli and cook for 5 minutes, or until the broccoli is tender. Remove from the heat, divide among serving bowls and serve immediately.

Each serving provides
1559 kJ, 372 kcal, 36 g protein, 15 g fat (4 g saturated fat), 22 g carbohydrate (5 g sugars), 8 g fibre, 197 mg sodium

Fibre fact

This Indonesian-style curry is delicious served with steamed rice. To increase the fibre, use brown rice instead of white.

Moroccan braised chicken

PREPARATION 15 minutes, plus 10 minutes soaking   COOKING 30–35 minutes   SERVES 4

1/4 cup (45 g) dried apricots
1 cup (250 ml) boiling water
1 tablespoon olive oil
4 skinless, boneless chicken breasts
1 large onion, finely chopped
6 cloves garlic, crushed
2 celery stalks, thinly sliced
410 g (15 oz) can chickpeas, rinsed and drained
410 g (15 oz) can chopped tomatoes
2 teaspoons grated lemon zest
1 1/2 tablespoons lemon juice
2 teaspoons ground coriander
freshly ground black pepper
1 1/2 tablespoons chopped fresh coriander (cilantro) leaves

Each serving provides
1594 kJ, 38 kcal, protein 42 g, 15 g fat (4 g saturated fat), 19 g carbohydrate (10 g sugars), 7 g fibre, 304 mg sodium

Soak the apricots in the boiling water for 10 minutes, then strain, reserving the soaking liquid. Chop the apricots and set aside.

Heat the olive oil in a large, deep frying pan or flameproof casserole dish over medium heat. Add the chicken and cook for 3–5 minutes, stirring until golden brown all over. Remove to a plate.

Add the onion and garlic to the pan and cook for 5–7 minutes, stirring frequently, until the onion softens. Add the celery and cook for 3 minutes, then stir in the apricots and their reserved soaking liquid, the chickpeas, tomatoes, lemon zest, lemon juice and ground coriander. Season, to taste, then bring to the boil. Return the chicken to the pan, then reduce the heat to low, cover, and simmer for about 15–20 minutes, or until the chicken is cooked through. Check the seasoning and stir in the fresh coriander just before serving.

Fibre fact

This recipe is high in fibre thanks to the chickpeas and dried apricots. Wholemeal (whole-wheat) flat breads would be a great high-fibre accompaniment.

Pan-fried fish with braised lentils

PREPARATION 5 minutes COOKING 40 minutes SERVES 4

- 4 x 180 g (6 oz) skinless, boneless firm white fish fillets
- 2 tablespoons olive oil
- 2 tablespoons butter
- grilled lemon halves, to serve

Braised lentils

- 1 tablespoon olive oil
- 1 small onion, finely diced
- 1 carrot, finely diced
- 1 celery stalk, finely diced
- 1 1/3 cups (250 g) puy or small blue-green lentils, rinsed and drained
- 2 cloves garlic, crushed
- 1 cup (250 ml) salt-reduced chicken stock
- 1 bouquet garni
- 2 tablespoons tomato paste (concentrated purée)
- 3 tablespoons chopped fresh parsley

Each serving provides
2348 kJ, 561 kcal, 54 g protein (9 g saturated fat), 28 g carbohydrate (4 g sugars), 10 g fibre, 642 mg sodium

To braise the lentils, heat the olive oil in a saucepan over medium heat and sauté the onion, carrot and celery for 5–7 minutes, or until softened and lightly coloured. Add the lentils, garlic, stock, bouquet garni and just enough water to cover the lentils. Bring to the boil, reduce the heat to low and simmer for 30 minutes, or until the lentils are tender, stirring regularly and adding a little more water if required. (If there is too much liquid, increase the heat and gently boil to reduce the liquid.) Stir in the tomato paste and parsley.

Heat the olive oil and butter in a large non-stick frying pan over medium heat until the oil is just sizzling. Add the fish fillets and cook for 3 minutes on each side, or until just cooked through and golden. Serve on a bed of lentils, with grilled lemon halves on the side.

Fibre fact

Due to their smaller size and thick skin, puy (blue-green) lentils are among the highest-fibre legumes. Their nutty flavour goes well with fish and chicken.

Seafood gumbo

PREPARATION 15 minutes   COOKING 25 minutes   SERVES 4

Heat the olive oil in a flameproof casserole dish over medium–low heat. Add the onion and garlic and cook for 5–7 minutes, or until the onion softens. Add the capsicums, okra and pumpkin and cook for 5 minutes, or until the capsicums are tender.

Add the barley, Tabasco sauce and thyme. Pour in 3 cups (750 ml) water and bring to the boil, then stir in the spinach and tomatoes. Reduce the heat to low, cover, and simmer for about 10 minutes, or until the barley is tender.

Add the prawns to the dish, cover, and cook for 4–5 minutes, or until the prawns just start to turn pink. Divide among serving bowls and serve immediately.

Fibre fact

Most grains have their fibre in their outside layer. Barley is different, as its fibre is distributed through the whole grain. This means that even polished (or 'pearl') barley is a high-fibre food with a very low glycaemic index. The fibre in barley is a special type that has a cholesterol-lowering effect. In this gumbo, it is combined with the high soluble fibre content of okra, and insoluble fibre from the vegetables.

1 tablespoon olive oil
1 large onion, finely chopped
3 cloves garlic, crushed
1 green capsicum (bell pepper), seeded and diced
1 red capsicum (bell pepper), seeded and diced
1 cup (100 g) okra pods, sliced
750 g (1 1/2 lb) butternut pumpkin (squash), peeled and cut into cubes
220 g (1 cup) pearl barley
1 1/4 teaspoons Tabasco sauce
1/2 teaspoon dried thyme
500 g (1 lb) baby spinach leaves, chopped
250 g (1 cup) canned chopped tomatoes
500 g (1 lb) raw prawns (uncooked shrimp), shelled and deveined, tails left intact

Each serving provides
1922 kJ, 459 kcal, 36 g protein, 8 g fat (1 g saturated fat), 60 g carbohydrate, (11 g sugars), 11 g fibre, 317 mg sodium

Artichokes with lentils & beans

PREPARATION ***20 minutes*** *COOKING* ***45 minutes*** *SERVES 4*

Trim the artichokes by removing the tough outer leaves and discard the tough end stem to 2.5 cm (1 inch) below the base. Use a paring knife to peel the skin off the remaining stem. Halve the artichokes lengthwise, then scoop out and discard the chokes. Halve the artichokes again. Place the cleaned artichokes in a bowl and pour over enough cold water to cover. Add 1 tablespoon of the lemon juice and set aside.

Heat the olive oil in a flameproof casserole dish over medium heat. Add the onion and garlic and cook for 8–10 minutes, stirring regularly, until the onion is golden brown. Add the carrot and cook for 4 minutes, or until it starts to soften slightly.

Remove the artichokes from the water and add to the casserole dish with the lentils, carrot juice, thyme, and remaining lemon juice. Add 1 cup (250 ml) water and bring to the boil, then reduce the heat to low, cover, and simmer for 25 minutes. Add the beans, stir to combine, and continue cooking for a further 10 minutes, or until the artichokes, lima beans and lentils are tender. Remove from the heat, divide among serving bowls and serve with a little crumbled fetta on top.

Fibre fact

Not counting legumes, artichokes have the highest fibre content of all vegetables. Half a cup of chopped artichokes has over 7 g fibre, even more if you keep part of the stem when you prepare them.

4 large artichokes
1/4 cup (60 ml) lemon juice
1 tablespoon olive oil
1 small onion, finely chopped
3 cloves garlic, crushed
1 large carrot, diced
3/4 cup (195 g) red lentils, rinsed and drained
1 1/2 cups (375 ml) carrot juice
1/2 teaspoon dried thyme
300 g (10 oz) butterbeans (lima beans)
2/3 cup (100 g) crumbled low-fat fetta cheese

Each serving provides
2369 kJ, 566 kcal, 43 g protein, 11 g fat (3 g saturated fat), 75 g carbohydrate, (8 g sugars), 31 g fibre, 580 mg sodium

Fruity Moroccan vegetable tagine

PREPARATION ***25 minutes*** *COOKING* ***35 minutes*** *SERVES 4*

1 tablespoon olive oil
1 large red onion, finely chopped
4 cloves garlic, finely sliced
1 tablespoon grated fresh ginger
500 g (1 lb) butternut pumpkin (squash), peeled and cut into cubes
1 teaspoon ground cinnamon
1 teaspoon ground cumin
1 teaspoon ground coriander
6 green cardamom pods, split open and seeds lightly crushed
3 bay leaves
2 x 410 g (15 oz) cans chopped tomatoes
3 large carrots, thickly sliced
300 ml (10 fl oz) salt-reduced chicken or vegetable stock
1/3 cup (55 g) raisins
1/4 cup (30 g) dried cranberries
1 cup (100 g) whole okra, sliced
1 large red capsicum (bell pepper), seeded and chopped
410 g (15 oz) can chickpeas, rinsed and drained
1/3 cup (30 g) toasted flaked almonds
2 tablespoons chopped fresh flat-leaf parsley

Each serving provides
1751 kJ, 418 kcal, 12 g protein, 16 g fat (2 g saturated fat), 61 g carbohydrate (32 g sugars), 15 g fibre, 645 mg sodium

Heat the olive oil in a large saucepan over high heat. Add the onion and cook for 5–7 minutes, or until softened. Add the garlic and ginger and cook for a few more seconds, then add the pumpkin and cook for 1–2 minutes. Reduce the heat to medium, add the cinnamon, cumin, coriander, bay leaves, tomatoes and carrots. Add the stock and bring to the boil. Add the raisins and dried cranberries, then reduce the heat, cover, and simmer for 10 minutes.

Add the okra and capsicum to the pan, cover again, and leave to simmer for 5 minutes. Stir in the chickpeas and simmer, covered, for a further 5–10 minutes, or until all of the vegetables are tender but still retain their shape.

Remove from the heat, divide among serving bowls and scatter over the toasted almonds and chopped parsley before serving.

Fibre fact

Beans and chickpeas are an excellent source of fibre, even better when they are eaten with grains such as wheat (couscous) and brown rice. Canned versions are a convenient way of including them in the diet.

Mixed bean cassoulet

PREPARATION 20 minutes COOKING 55 minutes SERVES 4

Preheat the oven to 200°C (400°F/Gas 6). Heat the olive oil in a flameproof casserole dish over medium heat. Add the onion and cook for 5–7 minutes, or until it softens. Add the garlic and pumpkin and cook for a further 2 minutes.

Add the stock, tomatoes, tomato paste, bay leaves, thyme and both of the beans to the dish and stir well (the mixture may look slightly dry at this stage, but the pumpkin will produce extra juices as it cooks). Slowly bring to the boil, then cover the dish and transfer to the oven to cook for 25 minutes.

Meanwhile, to make the breadcrumb crust, mix together the breadcrumbs, nuts and parsley in a bowl. Remove the casserole dish from the oven and season, to taste. Scatter the breadcrumb mixture over the top and return to the oven, uncovered, for a further 20 minutes, or until the crust is lightly browned. Remove from the oven, divide among serving bowls and serve immediately.

Fibre fact

Traditional cassoulet is a rich, fatty, meaty dish containing only small amounts of fibre from the dried beans used. In this lighter version, extra beans and vegetables replace the fatty meats under the delicious crunchy topping, providing much more fibre than the original French dish.

- 1 tablespoon olive oil
- 1 onion, chopped
- 2 cloves garlic, crushed
- 1 butternut pumpkin (squash), peeled and cut into cubes
- 300 ml (10 fl oz) salt-reduced vegetable stock, simmering
- 410 g (15 oz) can chopped tomatoes
- 1 tablespoon tomato paste (concentrated purée)
- 2 bay leaves
- 2 sprigs of fresh thyme
- 410 g (15 oz) can butterbeans (lima beans), rinsed and drained
- 410 g (15 oz) can borlotti beans, rinsed and drained
- freshly ground black pepper

Breadcrumb crust

- 3/4 cup (75 g) dried wholemeal (whole-wheat) breadcrumbs
- 1/3 cup (50 g) mixed nuts, chopped
- 2 tablespoons chopped fresh flat-leaf parsley

Each serving provides
1778 kJ, 425 kcal, 17 g protein, 15 g fat (2 g saturated fat), 55 g carbohydrate (13 g sugars), 15 g fibre, 876 mg sodium

Herbed eggplant lasagne

PREPARATION **30 minutes** *COOKING* **1¼ hours** *SERVES* **4**

2 tablespoons olive oil

1 tablespoon fennel seeds

1 bay leaf

1 large onion, chopped

1 clove garlic, crushed

1 celery stalk, diced

1 carrot, diced

1 cup (100 g) roughly chopped mushrooms

3 tablespoons chopped fresh marjoram or 1 tablespoon dried oregano

6 fresh sage leaves, shredded, or 1 tablespoon dried sage

2 large eggplants (aubergine), cut into 1 cm (1/2 inch) cubes

finely grated zest of 1 lemon

2 x 410 g (15 oz) cans chopped tomatoes

freshly ground black pepper

12 sheets instant lasagne (about 250 g/8 oz)

500 g (1 lb) low-fat cottage cheese or ricotta

2 tablespoons plain (all-purpose) flour

1 egg

100 ml (3 1/2 fl oz) low-fat milk

1/8 teaspoon freshly grated nutmeg

2 tablespoons freshly grated parmesan

Each serving provides
2275 kJ, 543 kcal, 39 g protein, 16 g fat (4 g saturated fat), 60 g carbohydrate (16 g sugars), 14 g fibre, 311 mg sodium

Heat the olive oil in a large saucepan over medium heat. Add the fennel seeds and bay leaf and cook for a few seconds, pressing the fennel seeds with the back of a spoon to bring out their aroma. Add the onion, garlic, celery, carrot, mushrooms, marjoram and sage and cook for 10 minutes, stirring frequently, until the vegetables soften slightly. Add the eggplants and lemon zest, mixing well, and cook for a further 5 minutes. Pour in the tomatoes and season, to taste. Bring to the boil, then reduce the heat to low and simmer for 15 minutes. Remove from the heat and set aside; discard the bay leaf.

Preheat the oven to 180°C (350°F/Gas 4).

Put the cottage cheese, flour and egg in a food processor or blender and process or blend to make smooth purée. Add the milk and process again briefly to combine, then season with nutmeg, to taste.

Pour half of the eggplant mixture into a large (20 cm/8 inch), square, baking dish. Cover with the lasagne sheets in an even layer, then add the remaining eggplant mixture and top with the remaining lasagne sheets, overlapping the pieces neatly. Spoon the cottage cheese mixture over the top and finally sprinkle over the parmesan. Bake in the oven for about 45 minutes, or until the topping is set and deep golden. Remove from the oven and leave the lasagne to stand for 10 minutes before slicing and serving.

Fibre fact

Many pasta varieties are now available in wholemeal (whole-wheat) versions. For a higher-fibre lasagne, choose wholemeal instant lasagne sheets (you will need to bake the lasagne for about 10 minutes longer).

Speedy two-bean chilli

PREPARATION ***5 minutes*** *COOKING* ***30 minutes*** *SERVES 4*

2 tablespoons olive oil
1 large onion, sliced
1 large red chilli, seeded and chopped
410 g (15 oz) can chopped tomatoes
1 tablespoon hot chilli (pepper) sauce
2 tablespoon tomato sauce (ketchup)
2 cups (500 ml) salt-reduced chicken or vegetable stock
1 tablespoon chopped fresh flat-leaf parsley
1 tablespoon chopped fresh oregano
410 g (15 oz) can red kidney beans, rinsed and drained
410 g (15 oz) can cannellini beans, rinsed and drained
1 cup (160 g/about 1 corn cob) fresh corn kernels
$^{2}/_{3}$ cup (160 g) low-fat ricotta
2 tablespoons snipped fresh chives

Each serving provides
1278 kJ, 305 kcal, 13 g protein, 14 g fat (4 g saturated fat), 30 g carbohydrate (14 g sugars), 8 g fibre, 681 mg sodium

Heat the olive oil in a large frying pan over medium heat. Add the onion and chilli and cook for 5–7 minutes, or until the onion softens. Add the tomatoes, chilli sauce, tomato sauce, stock, parsley and most of the oregano, reserving a few leaves to use as garnish. Bring to the boil, then reduce the heat to low and simmer for 10 minutes, stirring occasionally.

Add the kidney and cannellini beans to the pan, then add the corn and stir to combine. Continue to simmer for 10 minutes, or until the mixture has thickened slightly.

Meanwhile, mix together the ricotta and chives in a bowl. Divide the two-bean chilli among serving bowls and serve with a few oregano leaves sprinkled on top and the ricotta on the side for guests to help themselves.

Fibre fact

Both kidney beans and cannellini beans provide more than three times the amount of dietary fibre found in many other fresh vegetables.

Caribbean vegetable stew

PREPARATION ***10 minutes*** *COOKING* ***20 minutes*** *SERVES 4*

Heat the olive oil in a large saucepan with a tight-fitting lid over medium heat. Add the onion, garlic, pumpkin, capsicum and bay leaf. Stir to combine, cover, and allow the vegetables to sweat for 5–7 minutes, stirring occasionally, until the pumpkin starts to soften slightly.

Add the tomatoes, black-eyed peas and corn and stir to combine. Add the stock, worcestershire sauce, Tabasco, sugar and vinegar and stir again, then cover and simmer for 15 minutes, or until the pumpkin is cooked through.

Remove the pan from the heat, divide the stew among serving bowls and sprinkle over the parsley to serve.

Fibre fact

Corn is high in fibre, providing amounts similar to the legume family. In this recipe corn is combined with other high-fibre foods such as black-eyed peas and vegetables. To increase the fibre further, serve with brown rice instead of white.

1 tablespoon olive oil
1 onion, sliced
2 cloves garlic, crushed
750 g (1½ lb) butternut pumpkin (squash), peeled and cut into cubes
1 red capsicum (bell pepper), seeded and sliced
1 bay leaf
410 g (15 oz) can chopped tomatoes
410 g (15 oz) can black-eyed peas, rinsed and drained
1 cup (160 g/about 1 corn cob) fresh corn kernels
300 ml (10 fl oz) salt-reduced vegetable stock
1 tablespoon worcestershire sauce
1 teaspoon Tabasco, or to taste
1 tablespoon dark brown sugar
1–2 teaspoons balsamic vinegar
chopped fresh flat-leaf parsley, to garnish

Each serving provides
1224 kJ, 292 kcal, 12 g protein, 6 g fat (1 g saturated fat), 60 g carbohydrate (17 g sugars), 15 g fibre, 535 mg sodium

Lentil & cashew nut roast with tomato sauce

PREPARATION 20 minutes   COOKING 1¾ hours   SERVES 4

1 cup (250 g) split red lentils

2 cups (500 ml) salt-reduced vegetable stock

1 bay leaf

1½ tablespoons olive oil

1 large onion, finely chopped

1 large or 2 small leeks, white part only, finely chopped

1 red capsicum (bell pepper), seeded and diced

100 g (3½ oz) mushrooms, finely chopped

1 clove garlic, crushed

1 tablespoon lemon juice

¾ cup (60 g) fresh wholemeal (whole-wheat) breadcrumbs

¾ cup (115 g) unsalted cashew nuts, roasted and chopped

¼ cup (7 g) chopped fresh flat-leaf parsley

⅔ cup (85 g) grated mature cheddar

1 egg, lightly beaten

Tomato sauce

1 tablespoon tomato paste (concentrated purée)

½ teaspoon paprika

410 g (15 oz) can chopped tomatoes

150 ml (5 fl oz) red wine or salt-reduced vegetable stock

¼ teaspoon dried mixed herbs

Rinse the lentils in a sieve under cold running water. Drain, then tip into a saucepan. Add the stock and bay leaf, bring to the boil, then reduce the heat to low, cover, and simmer for 15 minutes, or until the lentils are soft and pulpy and the stock has been absorbed. Stir once or twice towards the end of the cooking time to prevent the lentils sticking. Discard the bay leaf.

Preheat the oven to 190°C (375°F/Gas 5). Line the base of a 5 cup (1.25 litre) loaf (bar) tin with baking (parchment) paper.

Heat the olive oil in a large non-stick frying pan over medium heat. Add the onion and cook for 5 minutes, or until it softens. Remove half of the onion to a plate and reserve for the sauce. Add the leeks, capsicum, mushrooms and garlic to the pan and cook for 5 minutes, stirring occasionally, until the vegetables soften. Stir in the lemon juice and remove from the heat.

Tip the lentils and vegetables into a large bowl. Stir in the breadcrumbs, cashew nuts, 2 tablespoons of the parsley, then the cheese and egg. (The mixture should be warm, not steaming hot when adding the egg. If necessary, allow it to cool for a few minutes.) Spoon into the prepared tin, level the top and cover with a piece of lightly oiled foil.

Bake the loaf in the oven for 30 minutes, then remove the foil and bake for a further 30 minutes, or until a skewer inserted into the centre comes out clean. Remove from the oven and leave to cool in the tin for 15 minutes before carefully turning out and cutting into thick slices.

Meanwhile, make the tomato sauce. Put the reserved onion and remaining sauce ingredients into a small saucepan. Bring to the boil, then reduce the heat to low and simmer for 20 minutes, or until slightly reduced. Stir in the remaining parsley just before serving with the loaf.

Each serving provides
2646 kJ, 632 kcal, 31 g protein, 8 g fat (8 g saturated fat), 53 g carbohydrate (14 g sugars), 14 g fibre, 926 mg sodium

Fibre fact

This nutty alternative to meatloaf has ten times the fibre of a traditional mince-based variety. Serve with salad on the side for a balanced high-fibre meal.

Eggplant & bean casserole

PREPARATION 15 minutes COOKING 1½ hours SERVES 8

1 kg (2 lb) eggplants (aubergine)
1/3 cup (80 ml) olive oil
2 large onions, thinly sliced
4 cloves garlic, crushed
3 x 410 g (15 oz) cans whole tomatoes
1 bunch fresh sage, chopped
1 teaspoon fresh thyme leaves
410 g (15 oz) can kidney beans, rinsed and drained
410 g (15 oz) can chickpeas, rinsed and drained
8 sprigs fresh flat-leaf parsley, to serve

Roasted capsicum

2 large red capsicums (bell peppers), seeded and sliced
2 teaspoons olive oil
1 small clove garlic, crushed

Each serving provides
1012 kJ, 242 kcal, 10 g protein, 12 g fat (2 g saturated fat), 22 g carbohydrate (11 g sugars), 11 g fibre, 40 mg sodium

Preheat the grill (broiler). To make the roasted capsicum, cook the capsicum strips, skin side up, under the grill for 12 minutes, or until the skin blackens and blisters. When the capsicums are cool enough to handle, peel and discard the skin and slice the flesh into 5 cm (2 inch) strips. Combine the oil and garlic in a mixing bowl. Add the capsicums, tossing well to coat in the oil. Cover with plastic wrap and refrigerate for at least 1 hour, or up to 3 days.

Meanwhile, dice half of the eggplants. Slice the remaining eggplants and set aside until needed.

Heat 2 tablespoons of the olive oil in a large saucepan with a tight-fitting lid over medium heat. Add the onions and garlic and cook for 8–10 minutes, or until golden. Add the diced eggplants and cook for 20 minutes, stirring regularly, until softened. Add the tomatoes, cover, and cook for 20 minutes, then stir in the sage, thyme, kidney beans and chickpeas – you may need to add a spoonful or two of water if the mixture seems a little dry. Remove from the heat and set aside.

Heat the remaining olive oil in a large non-stick frying pan over medium–high heat. Add the eggplant slices and cook for about 5 minutes, turning occasionally, until they start to soften.

Preheat the oven to 180°C (350°F/Gas 4). Place a layer of the bean and tomato mixture in a large shallow casserole dish. Cover with a layer of the eggplant slices and a few strips of roasted capsicum. Add another layer of beans, then cover with alternating slices of eggplant and capsicum. Bake for about 30 minutes, then remove from the oven and allow to stand for 5 minutes before dividing among serving bowls and scattering the parsley on top.

Fibre fact

Because we usually eat the seeds and skin, eggplants (aubergine) are among the highest-fibre vegetables. Both eggplants and legumes contain a blend of soluble and insoluble fibre, giving you the benefits of both.

Tuscan-style baked polenta

PREPARATION 20 minutes   COOKING 45 minutes   SERVES 4

- 25 g (1 oz) dried porcini mushrooms
- 2 cups (500 ml) low-fat milk
- 2½ tablespoons olive oil
- 2 celery stalks, thinly sliced
- 3 cups (270 g) sliced button mushrooms
- ⅓ cup (50 g) plain (all-purpose) flour
- 2 teaspoons lemon juice
- freshly ground black pepper
- 410 g (15 oz) can borlotti beans, rinsed and drained
- 1 cup (190 g) coarse polenta (cornmeal)
- 2 eggs, lightly beaten
- ⅓ cup (35 g) freshly grated parmesan

Each serving provides
2176 kJ, 520 kcal, 25 g protein, 18 g fat (6 g saturated fat), 66 g carbohydrate (12 g sugars), 8 g fibre, 478 mg sodium

Preheat the oven to 200°C (400°F/Gas 6). Put the dried porcini mushrooms and 1 cup (250 ml) of the milk in a small saucepan. Bring just to the boil, then remove from the heat and set aside to soak.

Heat the olive oil in a large saucepan over medium heat. Add the celery and cook for 3–4 minutes, stirring occasionally, until softened. Increase the heat, add the button mushrooms and cook for about 3 minutes, or until lightly golden. Add the flour and cook, stirring, for 2 minutes, then gradually add the remaining milk and stir until the mixture just comes to the boil and thickens.

Strain the porcini mushrooms, reserving the milk. Add the milk to the pan, bring back to the boil, stirring constantly. Coarsely chop the porcini mushrooms and add to the pan and simmer for 2 minutes. Add the lemon juice and season, to taste. Remove from the heat and pour into a shallow ovenproof dish in an even layer. Scatter the borlotti beans on top and set aside.

To make the polenta, put 3 cups (750 ml) water in a saucepan and bring to the boil. In a medium bowl, mix together the polenta and 250 ml (1 cup) water, stirring to combine. Gradually add the polenta mixture to the boiling water, stirring constantly, and keeping at a gentle simmer for about 5 minutes, or until the polenta is smooth and thickened. Remove from the heat and briskly stir in the eggs and about half of the grated parmesan; season, to taste.

Pour the polenta mixture over the mushrooms and beans, sprinkle the remaining parmesan over the top and bake for 20 minutes, or until the filling is bubbling and the top is lightly browned. Divide the baked polenta among serving bowls and serve immediately with a green salad.

Fibre fact

Mushrooms contain mainly soluble fibre, the kind that helps to reduce cholesterol levels and moderate blood glucose. They also have a special kind of starch called beta-glucan, which is thought to reduce cancer risk.

Chilli bean & polenta bake

PREPARATION 15 minutes   COOKING 1 hour   SERVES 6

- 1 tablespoon olive oil
- 1 small onion, finely chopped
- 1 small red capsicum (bell pepper), seeded and chopped
- 2 cloves garlic, crushed
- 1 carrot, diced
- 1 small zucchini (courgette), halved lengthwise and thinly sliced
- 2 teaspoons chilli powder
- 1 teaspoon ground cumin
- 410 g (15 oz) can chopped tomatoes
- 410 g (15 oz) can black beans, rinsed and drained
- 410 g (15 oz) can red kidney beans, rinsed and drained
- 410 g (15 oz) can chickpeas, rinsed and drained
- 1 1/2 cups (280 g) coarse polenta (cornmeal)
- 1 1/2 cups (210 g) grated low-fat cheddar

Each serving provides
2161 kJ, 516 kcal, 27 g protein, 17 g fat (7 g saturated fat), 69 g carbohydrate (10 g sugars), 18 g fibre, 654 mg sodium

Heat the olive oil in a large non-stick saucepan with a tight-fitting lid over medium heat. Add the onion and capsicum and cook for 5 minutes, or until the onion softens. Add the garlic and cook for 30 seconds, then add the carrot, cover, and cook for 2 minutes, or until starting to soften. Add the zucchini, chilli powder and cumin and cook for a further 1 minute, then stir in the tomatoes. Bring to the boil, then reduce the heat to low and simmer, partially covered, for 15 minutes, stirring regularly. Add all of the beans and the chickpeas to the pan and cook for 2–3 minutes to heat through. Remove from the heat and set aside.

Preheat the oven to 200°C (400°F/Gas 6). To make the polenta, put 4 cups (1 litre) water in a saucepan and bring to the boil. In a medium bowl, mix together the polenta and 250 ml (1 cup) water, stirring to combine. Gradually add the polenta mixture to the boiling water, stirring constantly, and keeping at a gentle simmer for about 5 minutes, or until the polenta is smooth and not gritty. Remove from the heat.

Working quickly, spread half of the polenta in the base of a 20 cm (8 inch) square baking dish, about 5 cm (2 inches) deep. Spoon the chilli mixture over the polenta in an even layer, then scatter over most of the cheese (reserving 2 tablespoons). Spread the remaining polenta over the top, then the reserved cheese and cook in the oven for 20 minutes, or until the filling is bubbling and the top is golden brown. Remove from the oven and allow to stand for 15 minutes before cutting into portions and serving.

Fibre fact

Cheesy polenta forms the base and top of this zingy Mexican-style dish. This provides more fibre than serving the chilli with white rice or tortillas.

Red lentil & vegetable dal

PREPARATION 15 minutes   COOKING 30 minutes   SERVES 4

Put the onion, garlic, chilli, carrot and eggplant into a flameproof casserole dish or large saucepan over medium heat. Add the vegetable oil and 2 tablespoons water and heat until it starts to sizzle, then cover and cook for 5–7 minutes, or until the onion softens.

Add the cumin, curry powder and mustard seeds to the pan, stirring for 1 minute to combine. Add the lentils and stock, bring to the boil, then reduce the heat to low and add the zucchini and tomato. Cover and simmer gently for 15 minutes, then uncover for a further 5 minutes, by which time the lentils should have burst open and thickened the liquid.

Remove from the heat and divide among serving bowls. Serve with fresh coriander sprinkled over the top.

Fibre fact

Wonderfully aromatic lentil dishes are found throughout India, with the spices varying according to the region. This dal features typically Southern Indian flavours, with vegetable chunks adding to the complexity (and fibre content) of this delicious dish.

- 1 onion, chopped
- 2 cloves garlic, crushed
- 1 fresh green chilli, seeded and chopped
- 1 carrot, grated
- 1 eggplant (aubergine), chopped
- 1 tablespoon vegetable oil
- 1 teaspoon ground cumin
- 1 teaspoon mild curry powder
- 2 teaspoons black mustard seeds
- 3/4 cup (185 g) split red lentils
- 3 cups (750 ml) salt-reduced vegetable stock, simmering
- 1 zucchini (courgette), halved and sliced
- 1 large tomato, chopped
- 2 tablespoons chopped fresh coriander (cilantro) leaves

Each serving provides
944 kJ, 225 kcal, 14 g protein, 7 g fat (1 g saturated fat), 27 g carbohydrate (9 g sugars), 10 g fibre, 788 mg sodium

Salads

Beef niçoise salad

PREPARATION 15 minutes   COOKING 20 minutes   SERVES 4

350 g (12 oz) lean rump steak, trimmed
1/4 teaspoon dried herbes de Provence, or to taste
freshly ground black pepper
500 g (1 lb) small new potatoes, scrubbed
250 g (8 oz) green beans, trimmed
250 g (8 oz) broad beans
250 g (8 oz) cherry tomatoes, halved
1/2 cup (70 g) mixed pitted black and green olives
2 tablespoons snipped fresh chives
3 tablespoons chopped fresh flat-leaf parsley
2 tablespoons extra virgin olive oil
1 tablespoon red wine vinegar
2 teaspoons dijon mustard
3 1/3 cups (150 g) baby spinach leaves
4 cups (160 g) torn lettuce leaves

Each serving provides
1554 kJ, 371 kcal, 29 g protein, 15 g fat (3 g saturated fat), 30 g carbohydrate (4 g sugars), 9 g fibre, 167 mg sodium

Put the steak in a shallow dish and season on both sides with the herbes de Provence and pepper. Set aside.

Cook the potatoes in a large saucepan of boiling water for 10 minutes. Add the green beans and broad beans and cook for a further 2–4 minutes, or until all of the vegetables are just tender. Drain well, then rinse under cold running water and set aside to cool.

Combine the potatoes, beans, tomatoes, olives, chives and parsley in a large bowl. Set aside.

To make the salad dressing, combine the olive oil, vinegar, mustard and 2 tablespoons water in a screw-top jar. Season, to taste, and shake well to combine.

Heat a non-stick frying pan over medium–high heat and cook the steak for 3 minutes on each side, or until cooked to your liking. Remove to a plate; let stand for 5 minutes.

To serve, thinly slice the steak and add to the vegetables. Pour any juices from the steak that have collected on the plate into the dressing, then pour the dressing over the meat and vegetables; toss well. Arrange the spinach and lettuce leaves in a large bowl and spoon the steak salad over the top.

Fibre fact

This delightful warm salad has a blend of fibres from the broad beans and vegetables. To increase the fibre further, serve it with wholegrain bread and finish with fruit for a healthy lunch.

Salads

Beefy pasta salad

PREPARATION 20 minutes   COOKING 15 minutes   SERVES 4

Cook the pasta in a large saucepan of boiling water according to the packet instructions. Add the broccoli florets during the last 2 minutes of cooking, then drain well and set aside.

Meanwhile, preheat the grill (broiler). Grill the steak for about 4 minutes on each side, or until cooked to your liking. Slice the steak thinly across the grain.

To make the dressing, combine the yogurt, mayonnaise, vinegar and basil in a small food processor and process until smooth. Transfer the dressing to a large serving bowl.

Add the steak and any juices accumulated on the cutting board to the bowl with the dressing, then toss to coat. Add the pasta, broccoli, tomatoes and onion to the bowl and toss again. Divide among serving plates and serve immediately.

Fibre fact

Broccoli is one of the highest-fibre vegetables. Include the peeled, trimmed broccoli stalks to boost the fibre content of this dish. You will get even more fibre if you use wholemeal (whole-wheat) pasta shapes, instead of white.

250 g (8 oz) rotelle (wheel-shaped pasta) or fusilli (long, corkscrew pasta)

500 g (1 lb) broccoli florets

300 g (10 oz) lean sirloin steak, trimmed

500 g (8 oz) roma (plum) tomatoes, quartered

1 red onion, halved and thinly sliced

Dressing

1 1/4 cups (310 g) low-fat natural (plain) yogurt

1/4 cup (60g) low-fat mayonnaise

1 tablespoon balsamic vinegar

3/4 cup (25 g) fresh basil

Each serving provides
1806 kJ, 431 kcal, 34 g protein, 6 g fat (2 g saturated fat), 56 g carbohydrate (12 g sugars), 9 g fibre, 288 mg sodium

Roast pork & quinoa salad

PREPARATION 20 minutes   COOKING 25 minutes   SERVES 4

- 1/4 cup (80 g) apricot jam
- 2 tablespoons dijon mustard
- 1 teaspoon finely grated lemon zest
- 2 tablespoons fresh lemon juice
- 1 teaspoon chilli powder
- 1 tablespoon olive oil
- 500 g (1 lb) pork tenderloin, trimmed
- 3/4 teaspoon salt (optional)
- 1 cup (200 g) quinoa, rinsed and drained
- 3 pink grapefruits
- 8 cups (400 g) rocket (arugula)

Each serving provides
2151 kJ, 513 kcal, 38 g protein, 12 g fat (2 g saturated fat), 61 g carbohydrate (25 g sugars), 6 g fibre, 343 mg sodium

Preheat the oven to 200°C (400°F/Gas 6). In a large bowl, whisk together the jam, mustard, lemon zest, lemon juice, and 1/2 teaspoon of the chilli powder. Reserve 3 tablespoons of the jam mixture for the pork and stir the olive oil through the remaining jam mixture to dress the quinoa; set aside.

Place the pork in a small roasting pan and rub over 1/4 teaspoon of the salt, if using, and the remaining chilli powder. Roast in the oven for 15 minutes. Brush over the reserved jam mixture to coat all over, then roast for a further 10 minutes, or until the pork is cooked through but still juicy.

Meanwhile, in a large saucepan, bring 2 cups (500 ml) water to the boil. Add the quinoa and remaining salt and return to the boil. Reduce the heat to low, cover, and simmer for 12 minutes, or until tender. Drain well, then place in a large bowl with the remaining jam mixture and toss to combine.

With a paring knife, remove the skin from the grapefruits. Working over a bowl to catch the juice, cut between the membranes to release the segments. Add the grapefruit segments and 1/4 cup (60 ml) of the juice to the bowl with the quinoa.

To serve, arrange the rocket on serving plates and spoon over the quinoa salad. Thinly slice the pork and arrange over the top.

Fibre fact

Quinoa is a rarity among the grains – high in fibre and also high in protein. Here the fibre from the quinoa combines with high-fibre grapefruit and the rocket leaves for a salad that is satisfying as a balanced light meal.

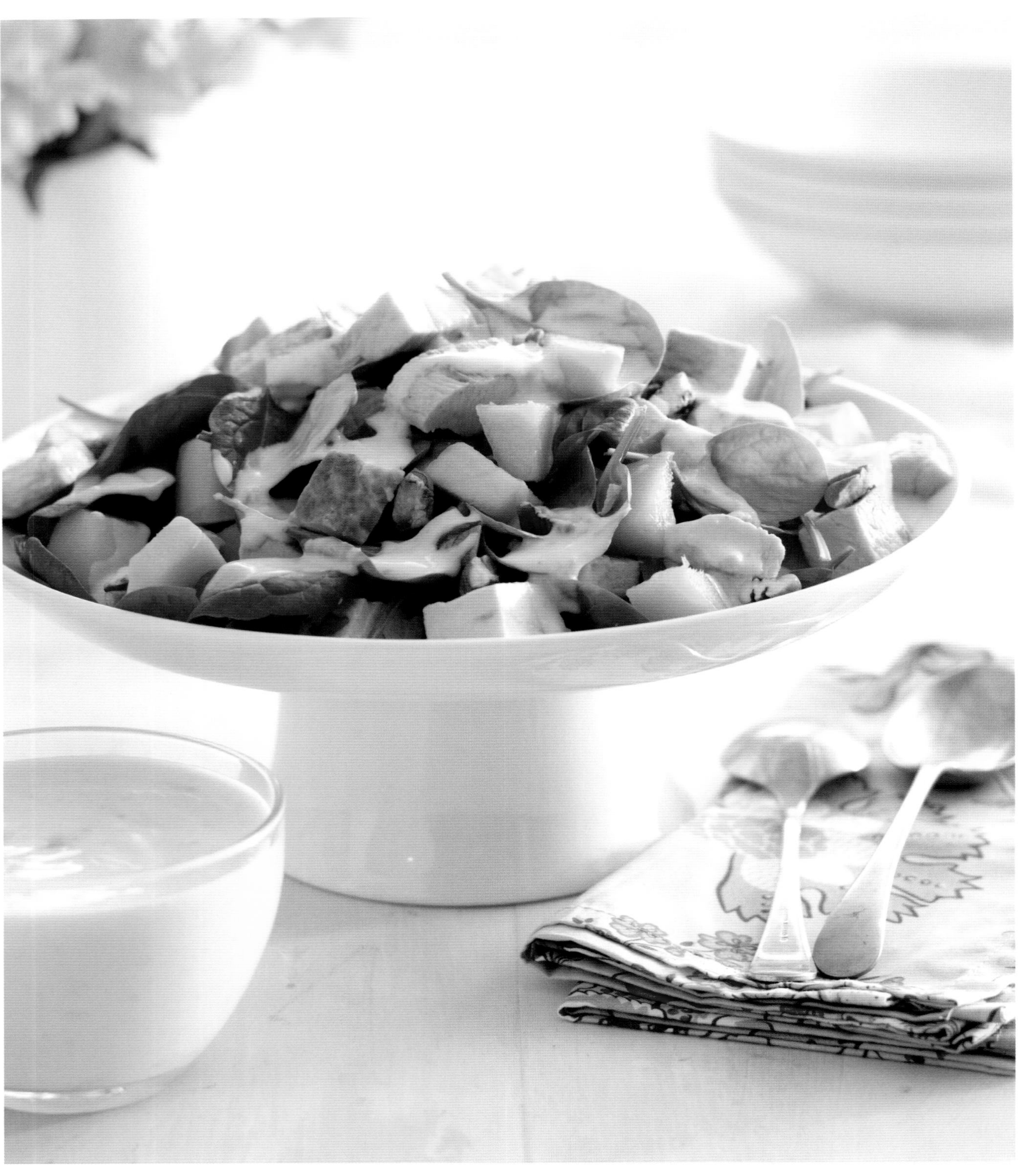

Turkey & mango salad

PREPARATION 10 minutes   COOKING nil   SERVES 6

In a large bowl, stir the yogurt, mayonnaise and chutney together until well combined.

Add the turkey meat and pecans to the yogurt mixture and stir well to coat. Gently fold in the mango and the spinach leaves. Toss gently to coat all of the ingredients.

To serve, divide the salad among serving plates.

Fibre fact

This salad is high in fibre thanks to the mango and greens. Serve with wholemeal (whole-wheat) bread to make a high-fibre lunch. It is a lovely way to use up leftover turkey or chicken, and you can vary the recipe by using other seasonal fruits such as peach, nectarine or apricot, instead of the mango.

200 g (7 oz) low-fat Greek-style yogurt

100 g (3 1/2 oz) low-fat mayonnaise

200 g (7 oz) spicy Indian mango chutney

600 g (1 1/4 lb) cooked turkey meat (from 1 medium hindquarter), cut into 2 cm (3/4 inch) chunks

1/2 cup (60 g) chopped pecans

2 large mangoes, peeled, stones removed and flesh cut into 2 cm (3/4 inch) cubes

2 cups (90 g) baby spinach leaves or rocket (arugula)

Each serving provides
1713 kJ, 409 kcal, 32 g protein, 17 g fat (4 g saturated fat), 31 g carbohydrate (28 g sugars), 3 g fibre, 578 mg sodium

Thai chicken & green papaya salad

PREPARATION 20 minutes COOKING 15 minutes SERVES 4

2 large cloves garlic
a pinch of salt
2 tablespoons unsalted roasted peanuts, coarsely chopped, plus extra, to serve
2 tablespoons dried shrimp
1 small lime
6 cherry tomatoes, cut into quarters
6 green beans, trimmed and cut in 2 cm ($^3/_4$ inch) lengths
2 small red birdseye chillies, halved lengthwise and seeds removed
400 g (14 oz) unripe papaya, shredded or coarsely grated
2 tablespoons grated palm sugar (jaggery)
1 tablespoon Thai fish sauce
$^1/_2$ tablespoon tamarind pulp
400 g (14 oz) skinless, boneless chicken thighs, cut into strips
1 tablespoon canola oil

Each serving provides
755 kJ, 180 kcal, 11 g protein, 7 g fat (1 g saturated fat), 24 g carbohydrate (18 g sugars), 7 g fibre, 582 mg sodium

Pound the garlic and salt together using a large mortar and pestle to make a smooth paste. Add the peanuts and dried shrimp and pound until evenly crushed.

Cut the lime in half and cut a thin slice from the middle, add this slice to the mixture and pound well to release the citrus oil from the peel. Juice the remaining lime and reserve the juice.

Add the cherry tomatoes and beans and pound briefly to bruise them, then add the chillies and pound briefly (the longer you pound them the spicier the flavour). Add the papaya shreds and pound briefly to bruise them and blend the flavours. Transfer to a mixing bowl, then add the lime juice, palm sugar, fish sauce and tamarind pulp and mix well with a wooden spoon. Set aside.

Put the chicken in a bowl and toss in the canola oil to coat. Cook in a chargrill pan or large non-stick frying pan over high heat for about 15 minutes, stirring occasionally, until golden all over. Remove from the heat and allow to cool slightly.

Toss the chicken with the green papaya salad and serve with the extra peanuts scattered on top.

Fibre fact

Green papaya salad is a popular street stall dish in Thailand, where it is ground with a mortar and pestle to order. If you don't have a mortar and pestle, just use a sharp knife to shred the garlic, shrimp, peanuts and chilli finely before you start. Green papaya is a high-fibre base for this salad, which is traditionally served with other high-fibre raw vegetables such as shredded cabbage. Green mango can also be used instead of the papaya.

Mexican chicken salad with salsa

PREPARATION 20 minutes   COOKING 15 minutes   SERVES 4

To make the salsa, combine the tomatoes, onion, chilli and coriander in a small bowl. Add the combined olive oil, lime juice and garlic and toss to combine. Set aside.

Place a chargrill pan or barbecue hotplate over high heat. Brush the chicken breasts with half of the olive oil. Cook for 5 minutes on each side, or until cooked through. Leave to rest for about 5 minutes, then thinly slice the chicken into strips.

Brush each tortilla with some of the remaining oil and cook for about 2 minutes on each side, or until lightly browned and crisp. Break into large pieces and set aside.

Put the enchilada sauce in a saucepan and bring to the a boil. Add the chicken and toss to coat, then remove from heat and cover to keep warm.

Chop or tear the lettuce leaves into small pieces and arrange on a large serving platter. Top with the kidney beans, avocado, pickled jalapeños and salsa. Arrange the chicken on top and sprinkle over the tortilla pieces. Garnish with parsley and serve.

Fibre fact

This tangy salad has fibre from the kidney beans and salad vegetables. To increase the fibre further, make your own tomato-based sauce for the chicken. Fry some finely chopped onion, garlic, long green chilli, and cumin powder. When the onion is tender, add chopped fresh tomatoes (with the skin and seeds) and simmer until the sauce is thickened – all this can be done while you are grilling the chicken for this recipe.

2 skinless, boneless chicken breasts or thighs

1 tablespoon olive oil

1/4 cup (60 ml) bottled enchilada sauce

4 large corn tortillas

1 large head cos (romaine) lettuce

410 g (15 oz) can red kidney beans, rinsed and drained

1 large avocado, stone removed and flesh diced

2 tablespoons chopped pickled jalapeños (hot chillies)

2 sprigs of flat-leaf parsley, for garnish

Salsa

2 large tomatoes, seeded and chopped

1 small red onion, finely chopped

1 fresh small red birdseye (Thai) chilli, finely chopped

3 tablespoons chopped fresh coriander (cilantro)

1/4 cup (60 ml) extra virgin olive oil

2 tablespoons lime juice

1 clove garlic, crushed

Each serving provides
2868 kJ, 685 kcal, 46 g protein, 43 g fat (8 g saturated fat), 29 g carbohydrate (7 g sugars), 10 g fibre, 568 mg sodium

Vegetable salad with tuna

PREPARATION 35–40 minutes   COOKING 15 minutes   SERVES 4

1¼ cups (160 g) frozen peas
150 g (5 oz) green beans, cut into 5 cm (2 inch) lengths
3 waxy potatoes, boiled, cooled and diced
1 yellow capsicum (bell pepper), seeded and thinly sliced
1 green capsicum (bell pepper), seeded and thinly sliced
1 white onion, thinly sliced
2 large tomatoes, seeded and cut into small wedges
⅔ cup (115 g) green olives stuffed with pimento, halved
1 small clove garlic, finely chopped
⅓ cup (90 g) low-fat mayonnaise
1 tablespoon olive oil
2 tablespoons lemon juice
freshly ground black pepper
180 g (6 oz) canned tuna, drained
lemon wedges, to serve

Each serving provides
1084 kJ, 259 kcal, 17 g protein, 9 g fat (1 g saturated fat), 26 g carbohydrate (10 g sugars), 6 g fibre, 869 mg sodium

Put ½ cup (125 ml) water in a saucepan and bring to the boil. Blanch the peas and beans for 5 minutes, or until tender. Drain well, reserving the cooking liquid. Set aside to cool.

Place the peas, beans, potatoes, capsicums, onion, tomatoes and olives in a bowl.

In a separate bowl, combine the garlic, mayonnaise, olive oil, lemon juice and ¼ cup (60 ml) of the reserved cooking liquid. Stir together until smooth, then season, to taste.

Pour the mayonnaise mixture over the vegetables and toss gently to coat the vegetables in the dressing. Arrange in serving bowls and flake the tuna over the top. Serve with the lemon wedges on the side.

Fibre fact

This salad makes a lovely high-fibre lunch or side dish. To increase the fibre further, leave the skins on the potatoes and the seeds in the tomatoes, and serve with a wholemeal (whole-wheat) roll or crispbread.

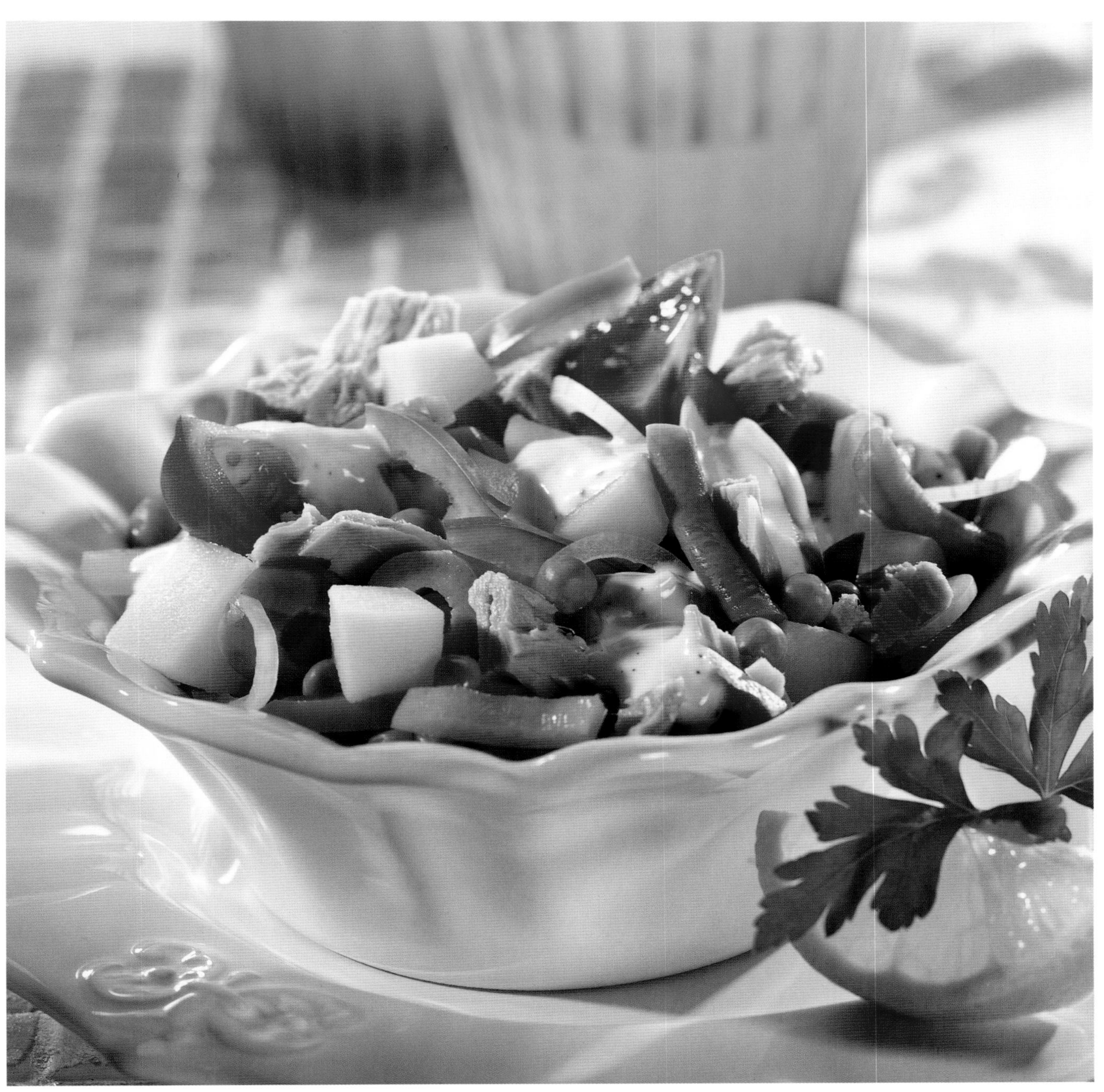

Crab & avocado salad

PREPARATION 20 minutes, plus 45 minutes soaking   COOKING nil   SERVES 4

Place the burghul in a large heatproof bowl with 2 cups (500 ml) boiling water. Let stand for 45 minutes, or until the grains are tender and all of the water has been absorbed.

Combine the olive oil, lemon juice, parsley, chives and tomatoes in a large mixing bowl. Mix in the burghul, then season, to taste. Set aside.

Combine the crabmeat, avocados, apples and bean sprouts in a bowl. In a separate bowl, mix together the mayonnaise, yogurt, lemon juice and cayenne pepper. Spoon over the crab mixture and toss very gently until just combined.

To serve, pile the burghul salad onto a serving platter and arrange the lettuce leaves on top. Spoon the crab salad onto the leaves and scatter over the walnuts. Serve immediately.

Fibre fact

Burghul (bulgur) is made from whole wheat kernels that have been pre-cooked and then dried before cracking into small fragments. As a whole grain food, it provides good amounts of minerals, B-group vitamins, and fibre, and makes a great basis for a satisfying salad.

1 cup (175 g) burghul (bulgur)
1 tablespoon extra virgin olive oil
1/4 cup (60 ml) lemon juice
3 tablespoons chopped fresh flat-leaf parsley
1 tablespoon snipped fresh chives
2 tomatoes, diced
freshly ground black pepper
350 g (12 oz) crabmeat, flaked
2 avocados, stones removed and flesh diced
2 sweet green apples, cored and thinly sliced
2 cups (180 g) bean sprouts
1/4 cup (60 g) low-fat mayonnaise
1/4 cup (60 g) low-fat natural (plain) yogurt
1 tablespoon lemon juice
a small pinch of cayenne pepper
small leaves taken from the hearts of 2 lettuces, such as cos (romaine) or iceberg
1/2 cup (50 g) walnut halves, roasted and roughly chopped

Each serving provides
2834 kJ, 677 kcal, 28 g protein, 43 g fat (7 g saturated fat), 43 g carbohydrate (16 g sugars), 14 g fibre, 435 mg sodium

Burghul & fish salad with lemon dressing

PREPARATION 15 minutes, plus 45 minutes soaking   COOKING 5 minutes, plus 1 hour chilling   SERVES 4

- 1 cup (175 g) burghul (bulgur)
- 300 g (10 oz) skinless, boneless ling, flathead or other firm white fish fillets
- 1 small lemon, thinly sliced
- 2 sprigs of flat-leaf parsley
- 5 black peppercorns
- 1 cucumber, seeds removed, diced
- 4 spring onions (scallions), thinly sliced
- 250 g (8 oz) cherry tomatoes, halved
- 2 tablespoons chopped fresh coriander (cilantro) leaves
- 2 tablespoons chopped fresh mint

Lemon dressing

- 2 tablespoons olive oil
- 2 tablespoons red wine vinegar
- finely grated zest and juice 1/2 lemon
- 1 teaspoon dijon mustard
- 1 clove garlic, crushed

Each serving provides
1260 kJ, 301 kcal, 20 g protein, 10 g fat (1 g saturated fat), 30 g carbohydrate (3 g sugars), 9 g fibre, 153 mg sodium

Place the burghul in a large heatproof bowl with 2 cups (500 ml) boiling water. Let stand for 45 minutes, or until the grains are tender and all of the water has been absorbed.

Meanwhile, place the fish fillets in a large non-stick frying pan. Add the lemon slices, parsley sprigs and peppercorns and pour in just enough cold water to cover. Bring to the boil, then reduce the heat to low, cover, and simmer for 5 minutes, or until the fish is opaque and flakes easily. Remove the fish from the pan and set aside to cool. Use a fork to flake the fish.

Put the burghul in a serving bowl and add the cucumber, spring onions, tomatoes and fresh herbs. Add the fish and toss gently to combine, taking care not to break it up.

To make the lemon dressing, whisk all of the ingredients in a bowl. Pour over the salad and mix gently to coat. Refrigerate for 1–2 hours to allow the flavours to develop before serving.

Fibre fact

Cucumber is a high-fibre addition to salads, especially with the skin and seeds. If the skin is very tough, rather than peeling it all off, you can use a zest cutter, or the point of a small knife, to remove thin strips of skin along the length of the cucumber leaving a stripy pattern. This is more palatable once chopped and keeps more of the skin's fibre and vitamins.

White bean salad with sesame dressing

PREPARATION 20 minutes, plus 12 hours soaking   COOKING 35 minutes   SERVES 4

1 cup (200 g) dried white beans
2 tomatoes, cored and diced
1 red onion, thinly sliced
2 green banana chillies (capsicums), seeded and sliced
1/3 cup (80 ml) extra virgin olive oil
1/3 cup (80 ml) red wine vinegar
freshly ground black pepper
2 hard-boiled eggs, peeled and sliced
1/3 cup (60 g) black olives
1/2 cup (15 g) fresh flat-leaf parsley leaves

Sesame dressing

1/3 cup (90 g) tahini (sesame paste)
2 tablespoons lemon juice

Soak the beans in a bowl of water overnight. Drain well, place in a saucepan and pour in enough water to cover. Bring to the boil, then reduce the heat to low and simmer for 35 minutes, or until softened. Allow to cool in the cooking water, then drain well.

To make the sesame dressing, combine the tahini, lemon juice and about 1/3 cup (80 ml) water in a bowl and stir until smooth. Set aside.

Put the beans in a serving bowl with the tomatoes, onion and chillies. In a separate bowl, whisk together the olive oil and vinegar and season, to taste. Pour over the salad and stir well to combine.

Just before serving add the eggs, olives and parsley to the salad and spoon the sesame dressing over the top.

Fibre fact

In this recipe, high-fibre white beans are combined with a dressing made from tahini, a sesame seed paste. If you can find it (try larger supermarkets and health food stores), brown or 'natural' tahini, made from unhulled sesame seeds, has more fibre than white tahini and a provides a nuttier flavour.

Each serving provides
2278 kJ, 544 kcal, 22 g protein, 38 g fat
5 g saturated fat, 25 g carbohydrate
(6 g sugars), 12 g fibre, 228 mg sodium

Pumpkin, lentil & goat's cheese salad

PREPARATION **10 minutes** *COOKING* **1 hour** *SERVES* 4

750 g (1 1/2 lb) pumpkin (winter squash), seeded and cut into chunks

2 tablespoons olive oil

1/2 cup (100 g) French-style green (puy) lentils

1/2 cup (125 ml) salt-reduced vegetable or chicken stock

1 cup (50 g) rocket (arugula) leaves

5 sprigs fresh mint, leaves picked, plus extra, to garnish (optional)

1/2 cup (70 g) raw pistachios

1 tablespoon extra virgin olive oil

juice of 1/2 lemon

2 teaspoons sumac powder

freshly ground black pepper

125 g (4 oz) soft goat's cheese

Each serving provides
1910 kJ, 456 kcal, 20 g protein, 31 g fat (8 g saturated fat), 27 g carbohydrate (10 g sugars), 8 g fibre, 253 mg sodium

Preheat the oven to 220°C (425°F/Gas 7). Toss together the pumpkin and olive oil and arrange in a single layer on a baking tray. Bake for 25 minutes, or until soft and turning golden brown at the edges. Allow to cool.

Meanwhile, put the lentils in a large saucepan with the stock and 1/2 cup (125 ml) water. Bring to the boil, then reduce the heat to low, cover, and simmer for 1 hour, or until the lentils are soft and all of the liquid has been absorbed. Allow to cool.

In a large bowl, combine the pumpkin, lentils, rocket, mint and pistachios. Sprinkle the olive oil and lemon juice over, and scatter with the sumac; season, to taste. Using a large spoon, stir gently to mix all the ingredients.

Serve the salad in the bowl or on a large platter, with the goat's cheese crumbled over the top. Garnish with the extra mint if desired.

Fibre fact

Like most salads, this recipe is high in fibre, but the protein from the lentils, pistachios and cheese means that it is hearty and satisfying enough to be served on its own, or with bread, as a light main meal. To increase the fibre even further, leave the skin on the pumpkin. This method works best with thin-skinned varieties such as butternut pumpkin (squash).

Warm potato & lentil salad

PREPARATION 10 minutes   COOKING 1 hour   SERVES 6

2 cups (350 g) brown lentils
1 kg (2 lb) waxy potatoes, peeled and cut into large chunks
1/2 cup (125 ml) extra virgin olive oil
2 tablespoons red wine vinegar
1 cup (125 g) pitted black olives
1 tablespoon capers, chopped
2 cloves garlic, chopped
1 tablespoon lemon juice
2/3 cup (20 g) chopped fresh flat-leaf parsley
6 spring onions (scallions), sliced
freshly ground black pepper

Each serving provides
1988 kJ, 475 kcal, 19 g protein, 23 g fat (3 g saturated fat), 48 g carbohydrate (3 g sugars), 11 g fibre, 256 mg sodium

Rinse the lentils and drain well. Put in a saucepan with just enough water to come about 4 cm (1 1/2 inches) above the lentils. Bring to the boil, then reduce the heat to low and simmer for about 40 minutes, or until tender – you may need to top up with water. Drain well and set aside.

Cook the potatoes in a saucepan of boiling water for 20 minutes, or until tender. Drain and transfer the potatoes to a large bowl.

While the potatoes are still hot, add the olive oil and vinegar and stir through. Add the lentils, olives, capers, garlic, lemon juice, parsley, spring onions, and season, to taste. Toss gently until all the ingredients are combined, and serve warm.

Fibre fact

Warm salads make vegetables more tempting during the colder months. You can increase the fibre content of this recipe by leaving the skin on the potatoes and by serving it with leafy greens.

Lentil salad with fried onions & rosemary

PREPARATION 25 minutes, plus 1 hour chilling   COOKING 40 minutes   SERVES 4

2 cups (400 g) French-style green (puy) lentils
1 small sprig of rosemary
1 dried bay leaf
1/3 cup (80 ml) olive oil
2 tablespoons red wine or herb vinegar
1 tablespoon lemon juice
1 teaspoon finely grated lemon zest
1/2 teaspoon ground cumin
1 clove garlic, crushed
freshly ground black pepper
3 small cooked potatoes, peeled and diced
2 large tomatoes, cored and diced
2 large white onions, sliced into rings
1/2 cup (15 g) chopped fresh flat-leaf parsley

Put the lentils, rosemary and bay leaf in a saucepan with just enough water to cover. Bring to the boil, then reduce the heat and simmer for about 40 minutes, or until softened. Leave to cool in the cooking liquid, then drain well, reserving the cooking liquid. Discard the rosemary and bay leaf.

In a large bowl, whisk together 2 tablespoons of the olive oil with the vinegar, lemon juice and zest, cumin, garlic and 3 tablespoons reserved cooking liquid; season, to taste. Add the potatoes, tomatoes and lentils, stirring well to coat, then cover and refrigerate for 1 hour.

Heat the remaining oil in a large non-stick frying pan over medium heat and cook the onion rings until golden brown. Remove from the heat and keep warm.

Stir the parsley into the salad just before serving, divide among serving bowls and top with the warm onions, to serve.

Fibre fact

In this salad, the fibres and starches from the lentils and potatoes ensure that this salad is satisfying and warming, and the acid of the dressing (from the lemon juice and vinegar) helps to reduce the glycaemic index to provide long-lasting energy.

Each serving provides
2095 kJ, 500 kcal, 28 g protein, 20 g fat (3 g saturated fat), 53 g carbohydrate (7 g sugars), 17 g fibre, 25 mg sodium

Corn & wholegrain wheat salad

PREPARATION 20 minutes   COOKING 30 minutes   SERVES 4

Put 4 cups (1 litre) water in a saucepan and bring to the boil. Add the wholegrain wheat and the bay leaf, then reduce the heat to low and simmer for 15–20 minutes, or until the wholegrain wheat is tender and all the liquid has been absorbed. Discard the bay leaf and tip the wholegrain wheat into a mixing bowl.

Preheat the grill (broiler). Brush the corn cobs all over with 1/2 tablespoon of canola oil and grill for about 10 minutes, turning frequently, until tender and lightly charred in places. When cool enough to handle, cut the kernels off the cobs with a sharp knife. Add them to the wholegrain wheat in the bowl.

To make the dressing, whisk together the mustard, orange zest and juice, the remaining canola oil and the walnut oil; season, to taste. Drizzle the dressing over the warm wholegrain wheat and corn, and toss well to mix. Leave to cool completely.

Add the capsicum, mushrooms, cucumber, roasted walnuts and mint to the wholegrain wheat mixture and toss gently together. Taste and add more seasoning, if needed. Serve at room temperature, garnished with slices of egg and mint.

Fibre fact

Wholegrain wheat grains (or wheat berries) are available from health food stores and large supermarkets. The uncooked variety needs pre-soaking and takes up to 2 hours to cook, so if you can't find pre-cooked wheat berries, for a quicker alternative use pearl barley instead. Pearl barley will cook in boiling water in about 30–40 minutes.

300 g (10 oz) pre-cooked wholegrain wheat (wheat berries)
1 bay leaf
2 corn (sweetcorn) cobs
1 1/2 tablespoons canola oil
1 teaspoon dijon mustard
1/2 teaspoon finely grated orange zest
1 tablespoon orange juice
1 tablespoon walnut oil
freshly ground black pepper
1 red capsicum (bell pepper), seeded and diced
1 1/4 cups (115 g) sliced button mushrooms
1/2 cucumber, cut into small chunks
2/3 cup (65 g) walnuts, roasted
1 tablespoon chopped fresh mint, plus extra, to garnish
1 hard-boiled egg, peeled and sliced, to garnish

Each serving provides
1842 kJ, 440 kcal, 13 g protein, 25 g fat (2 g saturated fat), 42 g carbohydrate (3 g sugars), 10 g fibre, 53 mg sodium

Russian bean salad

PREPARATION 15 minutes COOKING 3 hours, plus cooling SERVES 4

$3/4$ cup (150 g) dried soybeans, soaked overnight
500 g (1 lb) small new potatoes, scrubbed and halved
2 French shallots (eschalots), thinly sliced
250 g (8 oz) peeled, cooked beetroot (beets), diced
500 g (1 lb) tomatoes, sliced
1 fennel bulb, thinly sliced
1 cup (55 g) rocket (arugula)

Dressing

$2/3$ cup (150 ml) low-fat sour cream
$2/3$ cup (150 g) low-fat natural (plain) yogurt
4 sweet and sour gherkins, finely chopped
2 tablespoons creamed horseradish
1 teaspoon caster (superfine) sugar
freshly ground black pepper

Each serving provides
1564 kJ, 373 kcal, 22 g protein, 14 g fat (5 g saturated fat), 37 g carbohydrate (19 g sugars), 15 g fibre, 412 mg sodium

Drain the beans and rinse under cold running water. Put in a saucepan and cover with fresh water. Bring to the boil and boil rapidly for 10–15 minutes, then partly cover and simmer for about $2\frac{1}{2}$ hours or until tender. Drain and leave to cool.

Put the potatoes in a saucepan of boiling water and simmer for about 15 minutes, or until just tender. Drain and leave until cool enough to handle, then cut into bite-sized cubes. Set aside.

Meanwhile, for the dressing, mix together the sour cream and yogurt in a large mixing bowl. Stir in the chopped gherkins, horseradish and sugar; season, to taste.

Add the soybeans and shallots to the bowl and stir into the dressing. Add the potatoes to the bean mixture, then gently fold in the beetroot.

Divide the tomatoes, fennel and rocket among serving plates. Spoon the soy bean salad on top and serve immediately.

Fibre fact

Soybeans have a higher protein content than any other legume, making them a good basis for a nutritious vegetarian dish such as this hearty Russian-style salad. The fibre in this salad comes from the soybeans, beetroot, potatoes and fennel, as well as the salad vegetables.

Sweet potato salad with orange dressing

PREPARATION 20 minutes   COOKING 20 minutes   SERVES 4

- 500 g (1 lb) orange sweet potatoes, peeled and thinly sliced
- 1/4 cup (60 ml) olive oil
- 1 tablespoon lemon juice
- 1 tablespoon orange juice
- 1 teaspoon honey
- freshly ground black pepper
- 250 g (8 oz) rocket (arugula), torn
- 1 navel orange, peeled and segmented
- 1 small red onion, thinly sliced
- 1/2 cup (60 g) raisins

Preheat the oven to 200°C (400°F/Gas 6). Toss the sweet potatoes in half of the olive oil and arrange on a lightly greased baking tray. Cook for about 20 minutes, turning once, until tender and lightly browned.

Whisk together the remaining oil, lemon juice, orange juice and honey in a small bowl; season, to taste. Taste the dressing and add 1 teaspoon lemon juice, if needed, to taste.

Toss the warm potatoes and dressing together to coat and transfer to a serving bowl. Add the rocket, orange segments, onion and raisins, toss to combine, and serve immediately.

Fibre fact

Sweet potato has up to twice the fibre of ordinary potato, and its glycaemic index is much lower. For 30% more fibre, leave the skin on the sweet potato when making this salad. This helps it to hold its shape after roasting, and conserves many of the vitamins found just under the skin.

Each serving provides
1191 kJ, 285 kcal, 5 g protein, 14 g fat (2 g saturated fat), 35 g carbohydrate (23 g sugars), 5 g fibre, 40 mg sodium

Spinach, sweet potato & shiitake salad

PREPARATION 10 minutes   COOKING 30 minutes   SERVES 4

500 g (1 lb) orange sweet potatoes, peeled and sliced
1 1/2 tablespoon olive oil
2 cloves garlic, crushed
350 g (12 oz) fresh shiitake mushrooms, stems discarded and caps thickly sliced
600 g (1 1/4 lb) English spinach leaves
1/3 cup (35 g) walnuts, roasted and chopped
1/2 cup (125 ml) red wine vinegar
1 tablespoon dijon mustard

Preheat the oven to 200°C (400°F/Gas 6). Toss the sweet potatoes in 2 teaspoons of the olive oil and arrange on a large baking tray. Cook for about 20 minutes, turning once, until tender and lightly browned. Set aside.

Heat another 2 teaspoons of olive oil in a large non-stick frying pan over medium heat. Add the garlic and cook until fragrant, about 30 seconds. Add half of the mushrooms and cook until they begin to soften, then add the remaining mushrooms and cook until all the mushrooms are tender, about 5 minutes.

Place the spinach leaves in a large bowl. Add the sweet potatoes and walnuts. Remove the mushrooms from the pan with a slotted spoon and add to the bowl.

Add the remaining oil to the frying pan with the vinegar and mustard and whisk over high heat until warm. Pour the dressing over the salad and toss to combine. Divide among serving plates and serve immediately.

Each serving provides
1132 kJ, 270 kcal, 8 g protein, 14 g fat (1 g saturated fat), 26 g carbohydrate (13 g sugars), 5 g fibre, 188 mg sodium

Fibre fact

Of all mushrooms, Asian varieties have the highest content of beta-glucan, a special starch with tumour-fighting properties. Here they are combined with high-fibre sweet potato, nuts and spinach for an excellent blend of soluble and insoluble fibres.

Bean & rice salad

PREPARATION 30 minutes, plus overnight soaking   COOKING 1½ hours   SERVES 4

3/4 cup (150 g) black-eyed peas, soaked overnight in cold water

1 1/3 cups (260 g) long-grain brown rice

2 carrots, thinly sliced

125 g (4 oz) green beans, cut into 2.5 cm (1 inch) lengths

410 g (15 oz) can red kidney beans, rinsed and drained

410 g (15 oz) can chickpeas, rinsed and drained

1 large tomato, chopped

1 small red capsicum (bell pepper), seeded and chopped

1 small red onion, chopped

1 tablespoon canola oil

1 tablespoon wholegrain mustard

2 teaspoons caster (superfine) sugar

1/4 cup (60 ml) red wine vinegar, or to taste

1 tablespoon chopped fresh thyme

1 clove garlic, crushed

freshly ground black pepper

Each serving provides
2364 kJ, 564 kcal, 24 g protein, 9 g fat (1 g saturated fat), 97 g carbohydrate (11 g sugars), 16 g fibre, 378 mg sodium

Drain the black-eyed peas and rinse under cold running water. Place in a saucepan and cover with cold water. Bring to the boil, then reduce the heat to low and simmer for 45–60 minutes, or until tender. Rinse well, drain, then set aside.

Put the rice in a saucepan, cover with water and bring to the boil. Reduce the heat to low and simmer for about 30 minutes, or according to the packet instructions, or until tender. Drain and set aside to cool.

Meanwhile, blanch the carrots in another saucepan of boiling water for 3 minutes. Add the green beans and blanch for 4 minutes, or until the vegetables are tender. Refresh under cold running water and drain.

Place the carrots and green beans in a mixing bowl and add the kidney beans, black-eyed peas, chickpeas, tomato, capsicum and onion.

In a small bowl, whisk together the canola oil, mustard, sugar, vinegar, thyme and garlic, and season, to taste. Drizzle this dressing over the bean salad and toss well to combine. To serve, gently fold the rice into the bean salad.

Fibre fact

Brown rice, with its outer bran layer intact, has three times the fibre of white rice and much higher levels of minerals and B-group vitamins. Its does take longer to cook, but it is worth the effort for its delicious nutty flavour and superior nutrition.

Wilted spinach salad with croutons

PREPARATION 15 minutes   COOKING 20 minutes   SERVES 4

Preheat the oven to 180°C (350°F/Gas 4). To make the croutons, place the bread on a baking tray and bake for 5 minutes, turning once, until golden brown and crisp. Rub the toast lightly with the cut garlic (discard the garlic). Cut the toast into cubes.

Heat 2 teaspoons of the oil in a large non-stick frying pan over medium heat. Add the onion and cook for 5 minutes, or until it softens. Add the mushrooms and cook, stirring occasionally, for 4 minutes, or until the mushrooms are softened. Transfer to a large bowl. Add the spinach and croutons and toss to combine.

Add the remaining oil to the pan with the stock and vinegar. Bring to the boil and cook for 1 minute, then pour the hot dressing over the spinach and toss well to coat. Divide among serving bowls and serve immediately.

Fibre fact

Leafy green vegetables are high in fibre, with more than 2 g in just 1/2 cup cooked spinach or silverbeet. In this recipe, spinach and mushrooms are combined with crunchy croutons, which are made from wholemeal bread for additional fibre.

125 g (4 oz) wholemeal (whole-wheat) crusty bread, cut into 3 three slices about 1 cm (1/2 inch) thick

1 clove garlic, halved

1 1/2 tablespoons olive oil

1 large red onion, sliced

250 g (8 oz) mushrooms, thinly sliced

1 kg (2 lb) English spinach leaves, torn into bite-sized pieces

2/3 cup (150 ml) salt-reduced chicken stock

1 tablespoon balsamic vinegar

Each serving provides
872 kJ, 208 kcal, 14 g protein, 10 g fat (1 g saturated fat), 14 g carbohydrate (5 g sugars), 13 g fibre, 240 mg sodium

Middle Eastern bread salad

PREPARATION **20 minutes** *COOKING* **5 minutes** *SERVES* 6

1 telegraph (long) cucumber, seeded and diced

3 tomatoes, seeded and diced

6 spring onions (scallions), finely chopped

salt, for sprinkling

1 small iceberg lettuce, roughly chopped

3 small pita breads

2 tablespoons olive oil

freshly ground black pepper

Dressing

1/3 cup (80 ml) extra virgin olive oil

juice and finely grated zest of 1 lemon

2 cloves garlic, crushed

2 tablespoons chopped fresh flat-leaf parsley

2 tablespoons chopped fresh mint leaves

2 tablespoons chopped fresh coriander (cilantro) leaves

Each serving provides
1061 kJ, 253 kcal, 4 g protein, 19 g fat (3 g saturated fat), 16 g carbohydrate (4 g sugars), 4 g fibre, 152 mg sodium

Combine the cucumber, tomatoes and spring onions in a colander and sprinkle with salt. Leave for 10 minutes to drain. Place in a serving bowl with the lettuce.

Roughly tear the pita breads into small pieces. Heat the oil in a large non-stick frying pan over medium heat. Cook the bread for about 5 minutes, stirring often, until golden brown. Drain on paper towel to remove any excess oil.

To make the dressing, whisk all of the ingredients in a small bowl until well combined. Drizzle over the salad and toss well to coat; season, to taste. Top with pieces of pita bread and serve.

Fibre fact

This salad, known as fattoush, is a traditional accompaniment to a Middle Eastern meal. You can increase the fibre content of this recipe by choosing wholemeal (whole-wheat) pita bread, and by leaving the skin on the cucumber.

Salads

Goat's cheese & watermelon pasta salad

PREPARATION 15 minutes   COOKING 15 minutes   SERVES 4

Cook the pasta in boiling water according to the packet instructions. Rinse under cold running water, then drain and set aside to cool.

To make the mint dressing, put all of the ingredients in a screw-top jar and shake well to combine; season, to taste.

Crumble the goat's cheese into the cooled pasta and add the watermelon. Pour the dressing over and lightly toss together, then add the rocket and pine nuts.

To serve, toss the salad with the witlof leaves and prosciutto together in a bowl. Alternatively, arrange the witlof leaves on a serving platter, spoon the salad over the top and scatter over the prosciutto.

Fibre fact

This salad is particularly high in fibre thanks to the salad greens, watermelon, pine nuts and wholemeal (whole-wheat) pasta. Witlof (Belgian endive) is an excellent source of soluble fibre and is prized for its slightly bitter flavour, which helps to balance the sweetness of the watermelon in this salad. Be sure to store witlof away from light as this makes it darker and even more bitter.

200 g (7 oz) wholemeal (whole-wheat) penne

1 cup (120 g) crumbled goat's cheese

1/2 small watermelon, peeled, seeded and cubed

3 cups (100 g) rocket (arugula)

1/4 cup (40 g) pine nuts, toasted

2 small heads witlof (Belgian endive), leaves separated

4 slices prosciutto, trimmed and sliced

Mint dressing

2 1/2 tablespoons mild olive oil

1 tablespoon lime juice

1 tablespoon balsamic vinegar

1 tablespoon chopped fresh mint

freshly ground black pepper

Each serving provides
2300 kJ, 550 kcal, 17 g protein, 27 g fat (6 g saturated fat), 58 g carbohydrate (27 g sugars), 9 g fibre, 355 mg sodium

Roquefort & pear salad

PREPARATION 20 minutes   COOKING nil   SERVES 4

1 celery stalk, thinly sliced

3 ripe pears (preferably red or pink-flushed), cored and thinly sliced

1 head witlof (Belgian endive), leaves separated

1 cup (50 g) baby salad leaves

1/4 cup (25 g) pecans or walnuts, roasted

100 g (3 1/2 oz) roquefort cheese or other blue cheese

4 slices pumpernickel or walnut bread, toasted

Poppy seed dressing

2 tablespoons walnut oil

1 tablespoon sherry or balsamic vinegar

1 teaspoon dijon mustard

1 teaspoon honey

2 teaspoons poppy seeds

Each serving provides
1714 kJ, 409 kcal, 10 g protein, 22 g fat (6 g saturated fat), 42 g carbohydrate (18 g sugars), 8 g fibre, 844 mg sodium

To make the dressing put all of the ingredients in a screw-top jar and shake until well combined. Set aside.

Put the celery and pears in a large bowl with the witlof leaves, salad leaves and nuts. Add the dressing and toss well to coat. Crumble the Roquefort over the salad.

To serve, place a slice of the toasted pumpernickel or walnut bread on each plate and pile the salad evenly over the top.

Fibre fact

Rye breads such as pumpernickel are one of the highest-fibre breads available, with a very low glycaemic index and good amounts of both soluble and insoluble fibres. Filled with the whole rye grains, pumpernickel has a sweet nutty flavour that is a great accompaniment to strong-tasting cheese.

Side Dishes & Snacks

Fennel & potato with caramelised onions

PREPARATION 15 minutes   COOKING 1 hour   SERVES 4

500 g (1 lb) all-purpose potatoes
800 g (1$^{3}/_{4}$ lb) fennel
3 teaspoons olive oil
2 large onions, finely chopped
2 cloves garlic, crushed
freshly ground black pepper

Each serving provides
741 kJ, 177 kcal, 6 g protein, 4 g fat (<1 g saturated fat), 28 g carbohydrate (11 g sugars), 9 g fibre, 91 mg sodium

Cook the potatoes in a large saucepan of boiling water for 30 minutes, or until tender. Drain and, when cool enough to handle, peel and thinly slice.

Meanwhile, cut off the fennel stalks and fronds. Finely chop $^{1}/_{4}$ cup of the fronds and reserve; discarding the stalks. Cut the bulbs in half lengthwise and thinly slice. Set aside.

Heat the olive oil in a large non-stick frying pan over medium heat. Add the onions and garlic and cook for 8–10 minutes, or until the onions are golden brown.

Add the sliced fennel to the pan and cook, stirring, for about 10 minutes, or until just tender. Add the potatoes, season, to taste, and cook, stirring frequently, for a further 10 minutes, or until the potatoes and fennel are tender. Stir in the chopped fennel fronds, transfer to a serving bowl and serve immediately.

Fibre fact

Fennel has traditionally be considered to have gut-soothing properties, and its stringy celery-like structure gives it a high fibre content, with good amounts of both soluble and insoluble fibre. You can increase the fibre in this recipe further by keeping the skin on the potatoes.

Roasted potatoes & root vegetables

PREPARATION 10 minutes   COOKING 45 minutes   SERVES 6

Preheat the oven to 220°C (425°F/Gas 6–7). Wash and scrub all of the vegetables, then pat dry with paper towel. Peel the potatoes and cut each in half. Trim the carrots and parsnips, then peel them and cut them in half lengthwise. Peel the swedes and cut into quarters. Leave the beetroot whole with the skin on.

Place all of the prepared vegetables into a large roasting pan, add a good splash of olive oil and season, to taste. Roast for 30 minutes, then turn the vegetables over and roast for a further 15 minutes, or until golden and tender. Serve hot.

Fibre fact

You can leave the skins on all of these vegetables for added fibre – simply scrub very well before slicing them. The nutrients in most vegetables are more concentrated just under the surface, so eating them unpeeled means you get significantly more vitamins and minerals as well as more fibre.

4 roasting potatoes
3 carrots
3 parsnips
3 small swedes (rutabaga) or turnips
3 beetroot (beets)
olive oil, for drizzling
freshly ground black pepper

Each serving provides
583 kJ, 139 kcal, 5 g protein, 2 g fat (<1 g saturated fat), 26 g carbohydrate (12 g sugars), 6 g fibre, 62 mg sodium

Roasted vegetables & butterbeans

PREPARATION 10 minutes   COOKING 20 minutes   SERVES 4

- 2 red onions, each cut into 8 wedges
- 750 g ($1^1/_2$ lb) butternut pumpkin (squash), cut into 2 cm ($^3/_4$ inch) chunks
- 2 tablespoons olive oil
- freshly ground black pepper
- 2 zucchini (courgettes), cut into 1 cm ($^1/_2$ inch) slices
- a few sprigs of fresh thyme
- 1 teaspoon ground cardamom
- $^1/_2$ teaspoon soft brown sugar
- $^1/_3$ cup (80 ml) orange juice
- 2 teaspoons balsamic vinegar
- 410 g (15 oz) can butterbeans (lima beans), rinsed and drained
- $^1/_3$ cup (90 g) low-fat sour cream

Each serving provides
1273 kJ, 304 kcal, 9 g protein, 13 g fat (3 g saturated fat), 39 g carbohydrate (12 g sugars), 10 g fibre, 186 mg sodium

Preheat the oven to 230°C (450°F/Gas 8). Put the onion and pumpkin in a large roasting pan and drizzle over $1^1/_2$ tablespoons of the olive oil. Season well and toss well to coat the vegetables, ensuring they are arranged in a single layer. Roast in the oven for 10 minutes.

Meanwhile, put the zucchini into a large bowl, add the thyme and drizzle with the remaining oil. Toss with your hands to combine.

In a small bowl, mix together the cardamom, sugar, orange juice and vinegar.

Remove the pan from the oven and turn over the pumpkin and onions. Add the thyme-coated zucchini and butterbeans to the pan and drizzle over the vinegar mixture. Roast in the oven for a further 10 minutes, or until the vegetables are tender and lightly charred.

Remove the vegetables from the oven and spoon into a warmed serving dish or onto individual plates. Top with small spoonfuls of sour cream before serving.

Fibre fact

Zucchini are part of the marrow family of vegetables. Because we usually eat the skin and seeds, zucchini provide a good amount of insoluble fibre that complements the soluble fibre from the butterbeans in this recipe.

Baked couscous tomatoes

PREPARATION 30 minutes   COOKING 25 minutes   SERVES 4

Preheat the oven to 200°C (400°F/Gas 6). Place the tomato shells in a single layer in a baking dish. Put the tomato seeds and scooped-out flesh in a sieve over a jug, and press with the back of the spoon to squeeze out the juices. Discard the seeds and flesh, reserving the juice.

Put the dried fruits in a small bowl with 1/3 cup (80 ml) of the tomato juice. Stir, well then leave to soak. Add enough stock to the remaining tomato juice to make 350 ml (12 fl oz); set aside.

Heat 2 teaspoons of the olive oil in a non-stick saucepan over low heat. Add the pine nuts and cook for 2 minutes, stirring constantly, until golden. Remove to a plate.

Add the remaining olive oil to the pan and cook the spring onions for 2 minutes, or until softened. Stir in the cumin and coriander and cook for a few more seconds. Pour in the tomato and stock mixture and bring to a rapid boil. Remove from the heat, then add the couscous in a steady stream, stirring constantly. Cover and leave to stand for 3 minutes.

Stir the fruit, pine nuts and parsley into the couscous, then season, to taste. Spoon the couscous mixture into the tomatoes and replace the tops. Bake in the oven for 15 minutes, or until tender. Rest for 5 minutes before serving with the yogurt on the side, if desired.

Fibre fact

Wholemeal (whole-wheat) couscous is available in health food stores and large supermarkets, and can be used in this dish to boost the fibre content. Burghul (bulgur) is another wholegrain alternative that has three times the fibre of white couscous.

8 large beef tomatoes, tops cut off and the insides scooped out with a teaspoon and reserved

1/2 cup (75 g) chopped dried apricots

1/3 cup (55 g) chopped dates

1/3 cup (40 g) sultanas (golden raisins)

300 ml (10 fl oz) salt-reduced vegetable stock, simmering

1 tablespoon olive oil

1/2 cup (80 g) pine nuts

4 spring onions (scallions), thinly sliced

1/2 teaspoon ground cumin

1/2 teaspoon ground coriander

1 cup (185 g) instant couscous

2 tablespoons chopped fresh flat-leaf parsley

freshly ground black pepper

1 cup (250 g) low-fat Greek-style yogurt or tzatziki (optional)

Each serving provides
2449 kJ, 585 kcal, 19 g protein, 21 g fat (3 g saturated fat), 78 g carbohydrate (38 g sugars), 10 g fibre, 444 mg sodium

Crunchy nut coleslaw

PREPARATION 10 minutes   COOKING nil   SERVES 4

200 g (2 2/3 cups) thinly shredded white cabbage

1 large carrot, coarsely grated

1/3 cup (40 g) sultanas (golden raisins)

4 spring onions (scallions), white and green parts chopped separately

2 tablespoons low-fat mayonnaise

2/3 cup (160 g) low-fat natural (plain) yogurt

freshly ground black pepper

1/4 cup (30 g) thinly sliced radishes

1/3 cup (50 g) unsalted roasted peanuts

3 tablespoons chopped fresh flat-leaf parsley or snipped fresh chives, or a mixture of the two (optional)

Each serving provides
644 kJ, 154 kcal, 7 g protein, 6 g fat (1 g saturated fat), 17 g carbohydrate (15 g sugars), 4 g fibre, 165 mg sodium

Mix together the cabbage, carrot, sultanas and white parts of the spring onions in a large bowl.

Stir together the mayonnaise and yogurt and season, to taste. Pour over the cabbage and carrot mixture and toss well to coat the vegetables.

Just before serving, stir in the radishes and peanuts and sprinkle with the spring onion greens and the parsley or chives, if using.

Fibre fact

Peanuts and sultanas add flavour, as well as fibre, to this salad. Although peanuts are actually part of the legume family, nutritionally they are classed with the tree nuts as they provide similar amounts of healthy oils and insoluble fibre. For extra fibre, choose peanuts that have been roasted in their skins.

Barley & vegetable salad

PREPARATION **20 minutes** *COOKING* **45 minutes** *SERVES* 4

- $1^1/2$ cups (330 g) pearl barley
- 3 teaspoons olive oil
- 1 yellow or red capsicum (bell pepper), seeded and sliced
- 1 zucchini (courgette), cut into 1 cm ($^1/2$ inch) pieces
- 3 cloves garlic, crushed
- $^1/3$ cup (10 g) fresh mint, chopped
- $^1/4$ cup (60 ml) lemon juice
- $^1/2$ teaspoon freshly ground black pepper
- 250 g (8 oz) roma (plum) tomatoes, cut into thin wedges
- 1 cucumber, peeled, seeded and thinly sliced
- $1^2/3$ cups (200 g) crumbled soft goat's cheese or fetta cheese

Each serving provides
1848 kJ, 441 kcal, 18 g protein, 16 g fat (8 g saturated fat), 54 g carbohydrate (4 g sugars), 11 g fibre, 207 mg sodium

Put 3 cups (750 ml) water in a large saucepan and bring to the boil. Add the barley and cook for 45 minutes, or until tender. Drain well and set aside.

Meanwhile, heat 2 teaspoons of the olive oil in a large non-stick frying pan over medium heat. Add the capsicum, zucchini and garlic and cook for 5 minutes, stirring frequently, until the capsicum is just tender. Remove from the heat and allow to cool.

Whisk together the mint, lemon juice, pepper and the remaining olive oil in a large bowl. Add the barley, cooked vegetables, tomatoes and the cucumber, tossing to combine. Add the goat's cheese and toss gently, then serve at room temperature.

Fibre fact

Pearl barley has been polished to remove the outer layer of the grain. This makes only a small reduction in the fibre content because, unlike other cereals, barley has lots of fibre throughout its grain structure, mostly the soluble kind.

Spiced barley & corn

PREPARATION 15 minutes   COOKING 55 minutes   SERVES 4

Combine the spring onions, coriander, ginger, garlic and 2 tablespoons water in a food processor or blender and process or blend until smooth.

Heat the olive oil in a large saucepan over medium heat. Add the capsicum and cook for 4 minutes, or until just tender. Add the spring onion purée and cook for 2 minutes, stirring well, then add the barley, stirring to coat.

Add the stock to the pan with the tomatoes, corn, ground coriander and 1/2 cup (125 ml) water. Bring to the boil, then reduce the heat to low, cover, and simmer for 45 minutes, or until the barley is tender. Remove from the heat and transfer to a large bowl to serve.

Fibre fact

Canned tomatoes have usually been peeled and seeded before canning. In most recipes calling for canned tomatoes, you can increase the fibre content by substituting fresh tomatoes, with their skins and seeds. The skin is usually not noticeable if you chop the tomatoes finely before adding them to the recipe.

4 spring onions (scallions), thinly sliced

1/2 cup (15 g) fresh coriander (cilantro) or flat-leaf parsley leaves

2 tablespoons grated fresh ginger

3 cloves garlic, crushed

3 teaspoons olive oil

1 green capsicum (bell pepper), seeded and diced

1 cup (220 g) pearl barley

1 cup (250 ml) salt-reduced chicken stock

1 cup (250 g) canned chopped tomatoes

2 cups (260 g/about 2 corn cobs) fresh corn kernels

1/2 teaspoon ground coriander

Each serving provides
1374 kJ, 328 kcal, 11 g protein, 6 g fat (1 g saturated fat), 56 g carbohydrate (5 g sugars), 13 g fibre, 216 mg sodium

Braised root vegetables with dried apricots

PREPARATION 20 minutes, plus overnight soaking   COOKING 1¼ hours   SERVES 2

½ cup (100 g) dried apricot halves
¾ cup (100 g) French shallots (eschalots)
100 g (3½ oz) carrots
100 g (3½ oz) swedes (rutabaga)
100 g (3½ oz) turnips
100 g (3½ oz) celeriac
100 g (3½ oz) parsnips
100 g (3½ oz) orange sweet potatoes
100 g (3½ oz) mushrooms
2 tablespoons olive oil
200 ml (7 fl oz) salt-reduced vegetable stock
200 ml (7 fl oz) orange juice
freshly ground black pepper
fresh flat-leaf parsley, to garnish

Each serving provides
1858 kJ, 444 kcal, 10 g protein, 20 g fat (3 g saturated fat), 56 g carbohydrate (45 g sugars), 15 g fibre, 556 mg sodium

Place the apricots in a bowl and cover generously with cold water. Leave them to soak for about 8 hours, or overnight until rehydrated. Drain well.

Preheat the oven to 180°C (350°F/Gas 4). Pull apart the shallots, allowing them to fall into their natural segments. If the shallots are large and not segmented, halve them lengthwise. Cut the carrots, swedes and turnips into 5 cm (2 inch) chunks. Cut the celeriac, parsnips and sweet potatoes into 6 cm (2½ inch) chunks. Quarter or halve the mushrooms, depending on size.

Heat the olive oil in a large flameproof casserole dish over high heat. Add the vegetables, stirring to coat them lightly in the oil, and cook over high heat, stirring frequently, for 5–10 minutes, or until the vegetables are browned. Add the vegetable stock and orange juice and bring to the boil. Add the apricots and season, to taste.

Transfer the dish to the oven and bake for 45–60 minutes, or until the vegetables are tender and the liquid has reduced to a reasonably thick sauce. Garnish with parsley and serve.

Fibre fact

Root vegetables are an excellent source of fibre, all the more if their skins are left on. To increase the fibre further, serve this dish with wholemeal (whole-wheat) bread and leafy greens.

Lemony beans

PREPARATION 15 minutes   COOKING 10 minutes   SERVES 4

- 375 g (3/4 lb) green beans, halved
- 375 g (3/4 lb) butterbeans (lima beans), halved
- 2 teaspoons olive oil
- 3 cloves garlic, crushed
- 1/4 cup (60 ml) salt-reduced chicken stock
- 1 teaspoon finely grated lemon zest
- 1/4 cup (60 ml) lemon juice
- 1 tablespoon chopped fresh dill
- 2 teaspoons unsalted butter

Each serving provides
356 kJ, 85 kcal, 4 g protein, 5 g fat (2 g saturated fat), 5 g carbohydrate (3 g sugars), 5 g fibre, 45 mg sodium

Steam the green beans and butterbeans in a steamer basket or colander set over a saucepan of boiling water for 6 minutes, or until just tender.

Heat the olive oil in a large non-stick frying pan over medium–low heat. Add the garlic and cook for 2 minutes, or until softened. Add the stock, lemon zest and lemon juice and bring to the boil. Add the beans and cook for 2 minutes, or until heated through and well coated. Add the dill, remove from the heat, and stir in the butter until just melted; serve immediately.

Fibre fact

Green and butterbean pods contain both soluble and insoluble fibre and their refreshing sweetness and crisp texture make them a great accompaniment to other dishes. Make sure you do not overcook the beans or they lose colour, flavour and vitamins.

Warm grilled mixed vegetable salad

PREPARATION ***20 minutes*** *COOKING* ***15 minutes*** *SERVES 4*

Preheat a chargrill pan or barbecue hotplate to high. In a large bowl, mix together the capsicums, zucchini, onion, eggplants, mushrooms and 1 tablespoon of the olive oil. Cook the vegetables for about 15 minutes, or until brown and tender, turning occasionally to make sure they cook evenly.

Place the warm vegetables in a serving bowl. Add the radicchio leaves, olives, vinegar, oregano and remaining olive oil and toss gently to combine, then serve immediately.

Fibre fact

This salad combines a variety of high-fibre vegetables that are usually eaten with their skins, such as capsicums (bell peppers), zucchini (courgette) and eggplant (aubergine). Grilling them brings out their rich sweetness and gives them a creamy texture that contrasts well with the crisp bitterness of radicchio.

500 g (1 lb) green capsicums (bell peppers), seeded and thickly sliced

500 g (1 lb) red capsicums (bell peppers), seeded and thickly sliced

500 g (1 lb) zucchini (courgettes), thinly sliced lengthwise

1 large red onion, cut into wedges

6 baby eggplants (aubergine), thinly sliced lengthwise

150 g (5 oz) portobello or Swiss brown mushrooms, thickly sliced

1/4 cup (60 ml) olive oil

1 head radicchio, leaves separated

1 cup (125 g) pitted kalamata olives

2 tablespoons balsamic vinegar

1 tablespoon finely chopped fresh oregano

Each serving provides
1187 kJ, 283 kcal, 9 g protein, 19 g fat (2 g saturated fat), 19 g carbohydrate (12 g sugars), 8 g fibre, 370 mg sodium

Mediterranean stuffed vegetables

PREPARATION 25 minutes   COOKING 1¼ hours   SERVES 4

Put the rice in a saucepan with 2 cups (500 ml) water and bring to the boil. Reduce the heat to low and simmer, stirring often, for about 15 minutes, or until tender. Drain well and set aside.

Cook the lamb and onion in a non-stick frying pan over medium–high heat until the lamb is lightly browned and cooked through. Place a sieve over a bowl and tip the meat and onions into it. The fat will drip through and can be discarded.

Cut each capsicum in half lengthwise, keeping stalks intact, and remove the seeds. Cut the tops off the tomatoes and hollow them out, then chop the tops and tomato flesh and place in a bowl. Cut the zucchini in half lengthwise and hollow out the centres to leave 5 mm (¼ inch) thick shells, then chop the zucchini flesh and add it to the bowl with the tomato flesh.

Preheat the oven to 180°C (350°F/Gas 4). Heat the olive oil in a non-stick frying pan over medium heat. Add the garlic and chopped tomatoes and zucchini, and cook until they soften. Add the spinach and cook until wilted. Remove from the heat, add the rice, lamb, basil and egg to the vegetables and mix well to combine; season, to taste.

Spoon the stuffing into the vegetable shells. Arrange the capsicums and zucchinis in a single layer in a deep roasting pan. Cover with foil and roast for 15 minutes. Add the tomatoes and continue roasting for 15 minutes, or until the vegetables are almost tender. Uncover the vegetables and roast for a further 15–20 minutes, or until they are tender and the tops are lightly browned. Serve warm or cool, sprinkled with the extra basil.

Fibre fact

To increase the fibre content of this dish, you can replace the white rice with brown rice, increasing the cooking time to 30–40 minutes, or until the rice is tender.

½ cup (100 g) long-grain white rice
250 g (8 oz) minced (ground) lamb
1 onion, chopped
4 capsicums (bell peppers) of mixed colours
4 large beef tomatoes
2 large zucchinis (courgettes)
1 tablespoon extra virgin olive oil
3 cloves garlic, crushed
4 cups (180 g) baby spinach leaves
2 tablespoons shredded fresh basil, plus 2 tablespoons extra, to serve
1 egg, lightly beaten
freshly ground black pepper

Each serving provides
1460 kJ, 348 kcal, 23 g protein,13 g fat (4 g saturated fat), 33 g carbohydrate (12 g sugars), 8 g fibre, 98 mg sodium

Lentils with redcurrants

PREPARATION 15 minutes   COOKING 20 minutes   SERVES 4

- 1 cup (200 g) French-style green (puy) lentils
- 1 strip of orange or lemon zest
- 1 bay leaf
- 1 tablespoon raspberry vinegar
- 1 cup (150 g) redcurrants or blackcurrants
- 1 teaspoon honey
- 1 tablespoon canola oil
- 2 teaspoons hazelnut oil
- freshly ground black pepper
- 3 peaches, halved, stones removed and thickly sliced
- 4 cups (180 g) mixed salad leaves such as rocket (arugula) and baby spinach

Each serving provides
1030 kJ, 246 kcal, 15 g protein, 8 g fat (1 g saturated fat), 34 g carbohydrate (13 g sugars), 11 g fibre, 18 mg sodium

Put the lentils in a saucepan with the orange or lemon zest and the bay leaf, and cover with plenty of cold water. Bring to the boil, then reduce the heat and simmer gently for 15–20 minutes, or until the lentils are just tender but still firm to the bite. Drain well, discard the citrus zest and bay leaf. Place in a large bowl and set aside.

Combine the raspberry vinegar, redcurrants and honey in a small saucepan with 1/4 cup (60 ml) water. Bring to the boil and bubble for a few seconds, then remove from the heat. Lift out the redcurrants with a slotted spoon and add to the lentils. Whisk the canola and hazelnut oils into the redcurrant juices in the pan, and season, to taste. Drizzle the oil over the lentils and redcurrants in the bowl.

Add the peaches to the bowl and toss everything together gently, taking care not to break up the redcurrants and peaches too much. Arrange the salad leaves on serving dishes with the fruit and lentil salad spooned around. Serve the lentils and redcurrants at room temperature.

Fibre fact

Like other pulses, lentils provide fibre. They are also a good source of vitamin B_1 and niacin, both essential for helping the release of energy from food.

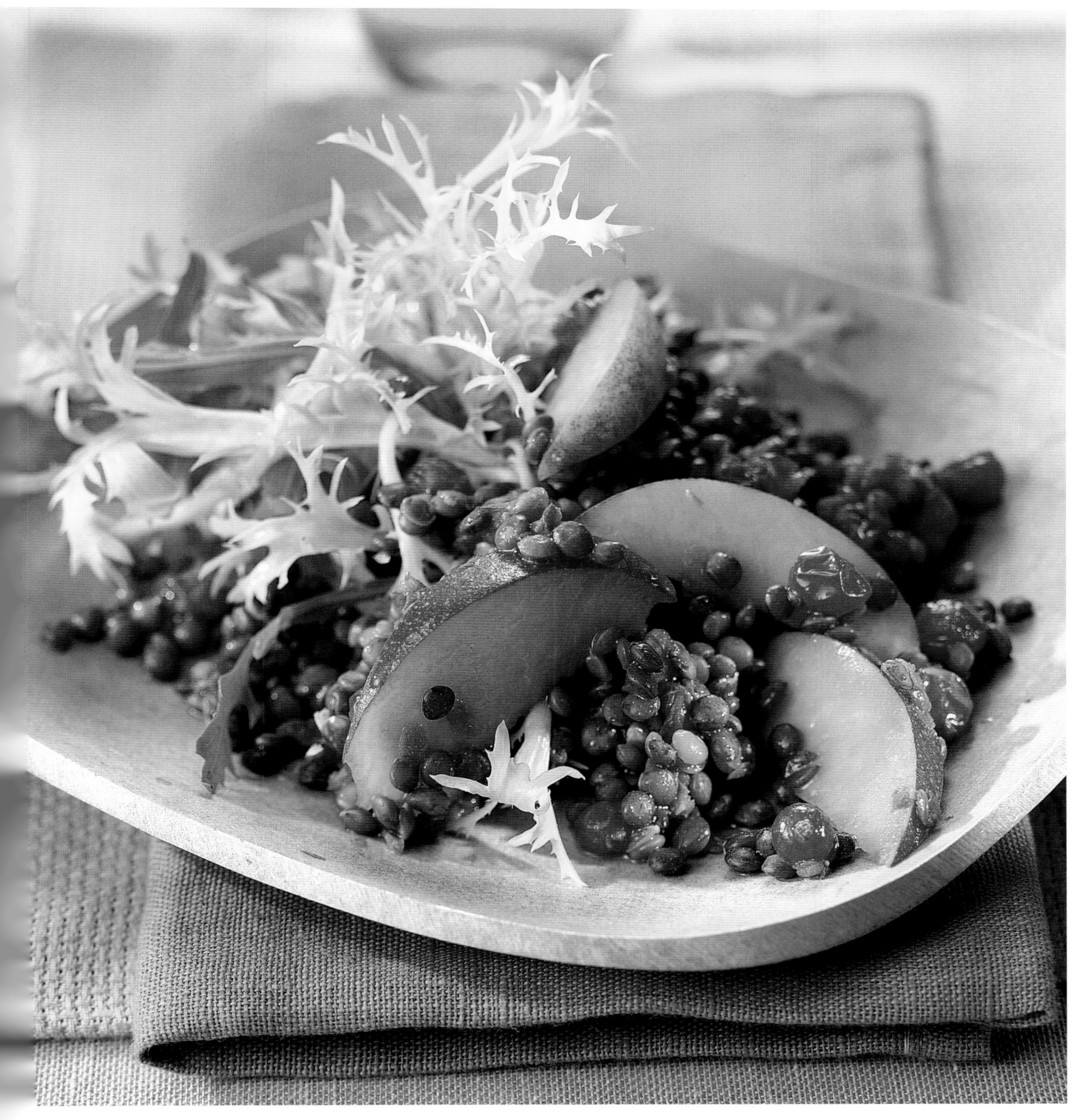

Persian-style couscous with roast vegetables

PREPARATION 20 **minutes** *COOKING* 35 **minutes** *SERVES* 4

Preheat the oven to 200°C (400°F/Gas 6). To make the roast vegetables, put the pumpkin and capsicums in a roasting pan with the squash, orange, bay leaves, cinnamon stick and garlic. Drizzle over the olive oil. Roast for about 25 minutes, turning once, until the vegetables are cooked through and tender. Remove from the heat and keep warm.

To make the couscous, heat the olive oil in a saucepan over medium heat. Add the onion and garlic and cook for 5 minutes, or until the onion softens. Add the dates, sultanas, cinnamon, ginger and wine, then cover and simmer for 5 minutes.

Remove the pan from the heat, stir in the couscous and chickpeas, then add 300 ml (10 fl oz) boiling water. Cover and leave to stand for 5 minutes. Add the mint, parsley and orange juice to the couscous and stir well to combine. Use a fork to fluff up the grains. Divide among serving plates and top with the roast vegetables. Serve warm or at room temperature.

Fibre fact

Dates are rich in potassium, niacin, copper, iron and magnesium. Both dates and sultanas are a valuable source of soluble fibre.

Roast vegetables

750 g ($1^1/_2$ lb) butternut pumpkin (squash), peeled and thickly sliced

1 red capsicum (bell pepper), seeded and cut into large pieces

1 yellow capsicum (bell pepper), seeded and cut into large pieces

250 g (8 oz) yellow (pattypan) squash, halved

1 orange, peeled and cut into large chunks

4 bay leaves

1 cinnamon stick, halved

2 cloves garlic, crushed

1 tablespoon olive oil

Couscous

1 tablespoon olive oil

1 onion, finely chopped

2 cloves garlic, chopped

$^1/_2$ cup (80 g) chopped pitted dates

$^1/_2$ cup (60 g) sultanas (golden raisins)

1 cinnamon stick

2 teaspoons grated fresh ginger

$^2/_3$ cup (150 ml) dry white wine

$1^1/_3$ cups (250 g) couscous

410 g (15 oz) can chickpeas, rinsed and drained

2 tablespoons chopped fresh mint

2 tablespoons chopped fresh parsley

juice of 1 orange

Each serving provides
2702 kJ, 645 kcal, 18 g protein, 12 g fat (2 g saturated fat), 116 g carbohydrate (38 g sugars), 13 g fibre, 201 mg sodium

White beans & silverbeet

PREPARATION 10 minutes   COOKING 25 minutes   SERVES 8

250 g (8 oz) silverbeet (Swiss chard)
2 tablespoons olive oil
1 small onion, finely chopped
1 carrot, peeled and finely chopped
1 teaspoon dried oregano
1 bay leaf
2 cloves garlic, crushed
1 cup (250 ml) salt-reduced chicken stock
3 x 410 g (15 oz) cans cannellini or butterbeans, rinsed and drained
freshly ground black pepper
1/2 cup (50 g) grated parmesan

Each serving provides
629 kJ, 150 kcal, 9 g protein, 7 g fat (2 g saturated fat), 11 g carbohydrate (3 g sugars), 7 g fibre, 493 mg sodium

Remove the tough stems from the silverbeet and finely chop the stems. Coarsely chop the leaves.

Heat the olive oil in a large non-stick frying pan over medium heat. Add the onion, carrot, oregano and bay leaf and cook for 5–7 minutes, or until the onion softens.

Add the garlic to the pan and cook for a further 30 seconds, then add the silverbeet stems and leaves, and the stock. Cook, stirring occasionally, for about 2 minutes, or until the silverbeet begins to wilt. Stir in the beans, cover, and simmer for a further 15 minutes, or until the silverbeet is tender and cooked through. Season, to taste, then remove and discard the bay leaf. Serve the silverbeet and beans with the parmesan sprinkled on top.

Fibre fact

This traditional Italian dish combines the insoluble fibre of silverbeet (Swiss chard) and the soluble fibre of legumes for a satisfying vegetarian dish that has good amounts of protein and iron. To make sure your body absorbs more of the iron, serve this dish with a tomato salad or some fruit, or use it as an accompaniment to meat.

Brown rice & chickpea pilaf

PREPARATION **10 minutes** *COOKING* **50 minutes** *SERVES* 4

1 tablespoon olive oil
1 large red onion, finely sliced
5 cloves garlic, thinly sliced
350 g (12 oz) green cabbage, sliced
3/4 cup (165 g) brown rice
410 g (15 oz) can chickpeas, rinsed and drained
410 g (15 oz) can chopped tomatoes
3/4 cup (90 g) raisins

Each serving provides
1541 kJ, 368 kcal, 11 g protein, 7 g fat (1 g saturated fat), 65 g carbohydrate (23 g sugars), 11 g fibre, 256 mg sodium

Heat the olive oil in a large saucepan with a tight-fitting lid over medium heat. Add the onion and garlic and cook for 5–7 minutes, or until the onion has softened. Stir in the cabbage, then cover and cook for 5 minutes, or until the cabbage begins to wilt.

Add the brown rice to the pan with 2 cups (500 ml) water and bring to the boil. Reduce the heat to low, cover, and simmer for 25 minutes, or until the rice has started to soften.

Stir the chickpeas, tomatoes and raisins into the pan and bring back to the boil. Reduce the heat and continue simmering for a further 10 minutes, or until the rice is tender.

Fibre fact

Not only is this pilaf a good source of carbohydrate, it is also low in fat and high in protein and a good source of folate. The high fibre content will keep you satisfied and stop you going back for more.

Eggplant & tahini dip (baba ganoush)

PREPARATION 20 hours, plus 1 hour chilling   COOKING 25 minutes   SERVES 4

500 g (1 lb) eggplants (aubergine)
1/2 cup (125 ml) lemon juice
1/4 cup (65 g) tahini (sesame seed paste)
1 tablespoon extra virgin olive oil
3 cloves garlic, crushed
2 tablespoons pomegranate seeds, to garnish (optional)
chopped fresh flat-leaf parsley, to garnish

Each serving provides
728 kJ, 174 kcal, 5 g protein, 15 g fat (2 g saturated fat), 4 g carbohydrate (4 g sugars), 5 g fibre, 20 mg sodium

Preheat the oven to 240° C (475°F/Gas 8–9). Place the eggplants on a baking tray lined with foil. Bake for 25 minutes, turning occasionally, until cooked through and softened.

Rinse the eggplants under cold running water to cool slightly, then cut each eggplant in half and scoop the flesh into a bowl, discarding the skin. Drizzle with 1/4 cup (60 ml) of the lemon juice. Use a fork to mash the eggplants slightly, then stir in the tahini, olive oil, garlic and 2 tablespoons of the lemon juice. Cover with plastic wrap and refrigerate for at least 1 hour.

Just before serving stir in the remaining lemon juice. Garnish with the pomegranate seeds, if using, and parsley to serve.

Fibre fact

Tahini (sesame paste) is a paste made from ground sesame seeds. Sesame seeds are a good source of both dietary fibre and monounsaturated fats.

White bean garlic dip

PREPARATION 15 minutes   COOKING 5 minutes   SERVES 8

Blanch the garlic in a small saucepan of boiling water for about 3 minutes. Drain well, reserving 2 tablespoons of the cooking liquid. Peel the garlic cloves.

Combine the garlic, reserved cooking liquid and cannellini beans in a food processor and process until smooth. Add the olive oil, lemon juice and coriander, and process briefly to combine. Use a spoon to fold through the mint and parsley by hand.

Transfer the mixture to a small serving bowl. Serve sprinkled with the paprika, if using.

Fibre fact

Many dips are made using sour cream as a base, which provides lots of extra fat without any fibre. Legumes make a fantastic alternative, much more nutritious and high in fibre.

- 10 cloves garlic (unpeeled)
- 2 x 410 g (15 oz) cans cannellini beans, rinsed and drained
- 1/3 cup (80 ml) olive oil
- 2 tablespoons lemon juice
- 1 teaspoon ground coriander
- 2 tablespoons chopped fresh mint
- 2 tablespoons chopped fresh flat-leaf parsley
- 1 teaspoon paprika (optional)

Each serving (¼ cup) provides
477 kJ, 114 kcal, 3 g protein, 9 g fat (1 g saturated fat), 5 g carbohydrate (1 g sugars), 3 g fibre, 103 mg sodium

Tabouleh

PREPARATION 30 minutes   COOKING nil   SERVES 4

- 3/4 cup (130 g) burghul (bulgur)
- 1 1/4 cups (310 ml) boiling water or vegetable stock
- 2 tablespoons extra virgin olive oil
- juice of 1 lemon
- 4 spring onions (scallions), thinly sliced
- 2 tomatoes, diced
- 4 cups (120 g) fresh flat-leaf parsley leaves, chopped
- freshly ground black pepper

Each serving provides
890 kJ, 212 kcal, 6 g protein, 10 g fat (1 g saturated fat), 24 g carbohydrate (4 g sugars), 10 g fibre, 463 mg sodium

Place the burghul in a heatproof dish and pour the boiling water over the top. Set aside for 20 minutes, stirring halfway through, until all the liquid has been absorbed – the burghul should be damp but not watery. If the liquid is not all absorbed, gently press the excess liquid out through a strainer.

Pour over the olive oil and lemon juice and stir well to combine. Add the spring onions, tomatoes and parsley and stir through, then season to taste. Serve at room temperature.

Fibre fact

This traditional Middle Eastern side dish makes a refreshing accompaniment to falafel or barbecued meats, as well as being an essential component of a mezze platter, where a variety of dips and small snacks are offered with flat bread. Both the burghul (bulgur) and the parsley are high in fibre and provide good amounts of iron.

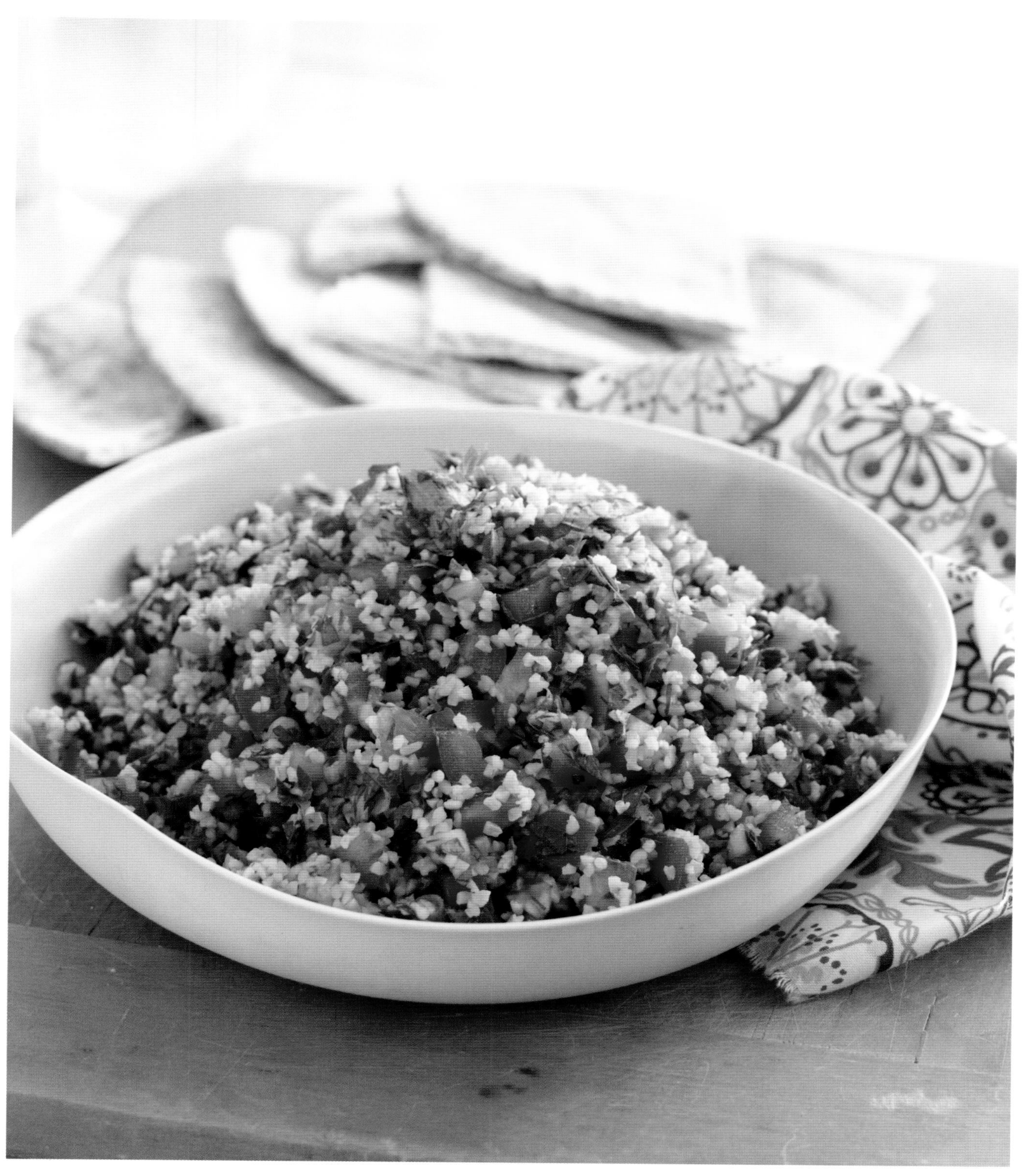

Hummus with pita crisps

PREPARATION ***15 minutes*** *COOKING* ***5 minutes*** *SERVES 4*

To make the hummus, put the chickpeas, cumin, garlic, lemon juice, olive oil and ricotta in a food processor. Blend for about 1–2 minutes or until very smooth, stopping to scrape down the sides with a spatula once or twice. Alternatively, you can place the ingredients in a large bowl and purée with a hand-held blender. For a slightly chunkier result, mash the chickpeas with a potato masher or fork until quite smooth, then stir in the other ingredients. Season, to taste, then spoon into a bowl. Cover and refrigerate until ready to serve.

To make the pita crisps, preheat the grill (broiler). Spread out the pita breads on a baking tray and lightly brush the top side of each using half of the olive oil. Sprinkle over half of the sesame seeds and grill for about 1 minute, or until both the bread and seeds are golden brown. Turn the pitas over, brush with the remaining olive oil and sprinkle with the remaining sesame seeds. Return to the hot grill and toast for 1 minute further, or until the bread and seeds are golden brown.

Using scissors, quickly cut the warm pitas into 2 cm (3/4 inch) strips and allow to cool and become crisp. The pita crisps can be kept in an airtight container for up to 2 days.

To serve, sprinkle the hummus with a pinch each of paprika and ground cumin, if using, then serve with the pita crisps and some lemon wedges on the side.

Fibre fact

There are many different variations on this popular Middle Eastern dip, which is sometimes flavoured with capsicum (bell pepper) or tahini (sesame paste). In this version, low-fat ricotta is used for an extra creamy effect and to provide more calcium. To increase the fibre further, serve the hummus with wholemeal (whole-wheat) pita breads.

Hummus

410g (15 oz) chickpeas, rinsed and drained

1/2 teaspoon ground cumin

2 garlic cloves, crushed

2 tablespoons lemon juice

2 teaspoons olive oil

2/3 cup (160 g) low-fat ricotta

freshly ground black pepper

paprika and ground cumin, to garnish (optional)

lemon wedges, to serve

Pita crisps

6 small pita breads

1 1/2 tablespoons olive oil

1/4 cup (40 g) sesame seeds

Each serving provides
1861 kJ, 444 kcal, 17 g protein, 20 g fat (4 g saturated fat), 48 g carbohydrate (2 g sugars), 6 g fibre, 604 mg sodium

Mexican rice with tomatoes & spices

PREPARATION ***15 minutes*** *COOKING* ***50 minutes*** *SERVES* ***4***

2 tablespoons canola oil

75 g (2 1/2 oz) chorizo, skinned and chopped

1 onion, finely chopped

2 cloves garlic, crushed

1 cup (200 g) long-grain brown rice, rinsed

2 x 410 g (15 oz) cans chopped tomatoes

2 teaspoons tomato paste (concentrated purée)

1 cup (160 g/about 1 corn cob) fresh corn kernels

3/4 cup (115 g) frozen peas, thawed

1 bay leaf

200 ml (7 fl oz) salt-reduced vegetable stock or water

1/2 teaspoon dried red chilli flakes

1/2 teaspoon sugar

freshly ground black pepper

8 sprigs of fresh coriander (cilantro)

4 lime wedges

4 flour tortillas

Each serving provides
2112 kJ, 505 kcal, 14 g protein, 18 g fat (4 g saturated fat), 72 g carbohydrate (11 g sugars), 7 g fibre, 572 mg sodium

Heat the oil in a large flameproof casserole dish or saucepan with a tight-fitting lid over medium–high heat. Add the chorizo and stir for 2 minutes. Add the onion and garlic and continue cooking for 3–5 minutes, stirring, until the onion softens and the chorizo is cooked.

Add the rice to the dish and stir for 1 minute, then stir in the tomatoes, tomato paste, corn, peas, bay leaf, stock, chilli flakes and sugar. Slowly bring to the boil, stirring occasionally, then reduce the heat to low, cover, and leave to simmer for 30–40 minutes, or until the rice is tender and all the liquid has been absorbed. Add a little more stock if the mixture becomes too dry before the rice is cooked; season, to taste. Remove from the heat and leave to stand, covered, for about 5 minutes.

Heat the flour tortillas under a hot grill (broiler) until warm. Serve the rice with coriander sprigs, lime wedges and tortillas.

Fibre fact

Brown rice, corn and peas provide most of the fibre in this dish. To increase the fibre further, serve with wholemeal tortillas and some salad greens on the side.

Dried fruit

PREPARATION ***5 minutes*** *COOKING* ***25 minutes*** *SERVES 6–8*

Rinse the prunes, figs, apricots and peaches and place in a large saucepan with 4 cups (1 litre) water. Scrape the seeds from the vanilla bean; add the seeds and the pod, the sultanas and orange zest to the pan. Partially cover the pan and bring to the boil.

Fully cover the pan and simmer for 5 minutes. Add the sugar and stir until dissolved. Re-cover and simmer over low heat for a further 15 minutes, then remove from the heat and allow to cool.

Add the orange flower water to the fruit. Transfer to a serving bowl, cover and refrigerate. Serve with the yogurt on the side.

Fibre fact

Dried fruits are a convenient base for a fruit salad when fruit options are limited. Drying does not affect the fibre content.

- 3/4 cup (140 g) pitted prunes
- 1/2 cup (100 g) dried figs
- 1 cup (135 g) dried apricots
- 3/4 cup (125 g) dried peaches or pears, halved
- 1/3 cup (55 g) sultanas
- 1 vanilla bean, halved
- 1 tablespoon julienned orange zest
- 1/2 cup (100 g) sugar
- 2 tablespoons orange flower water or rosewater
- 1 cup (250 g) low-fat natural (plain) yogurt, to serve

Each serving provides
889 kJ, 212 kcal, 3 g protein, <1 g fat (<1 g saturated fat), 50 g carbohydrate (46 g sugars), 7 g fibre, 19 mg sodium

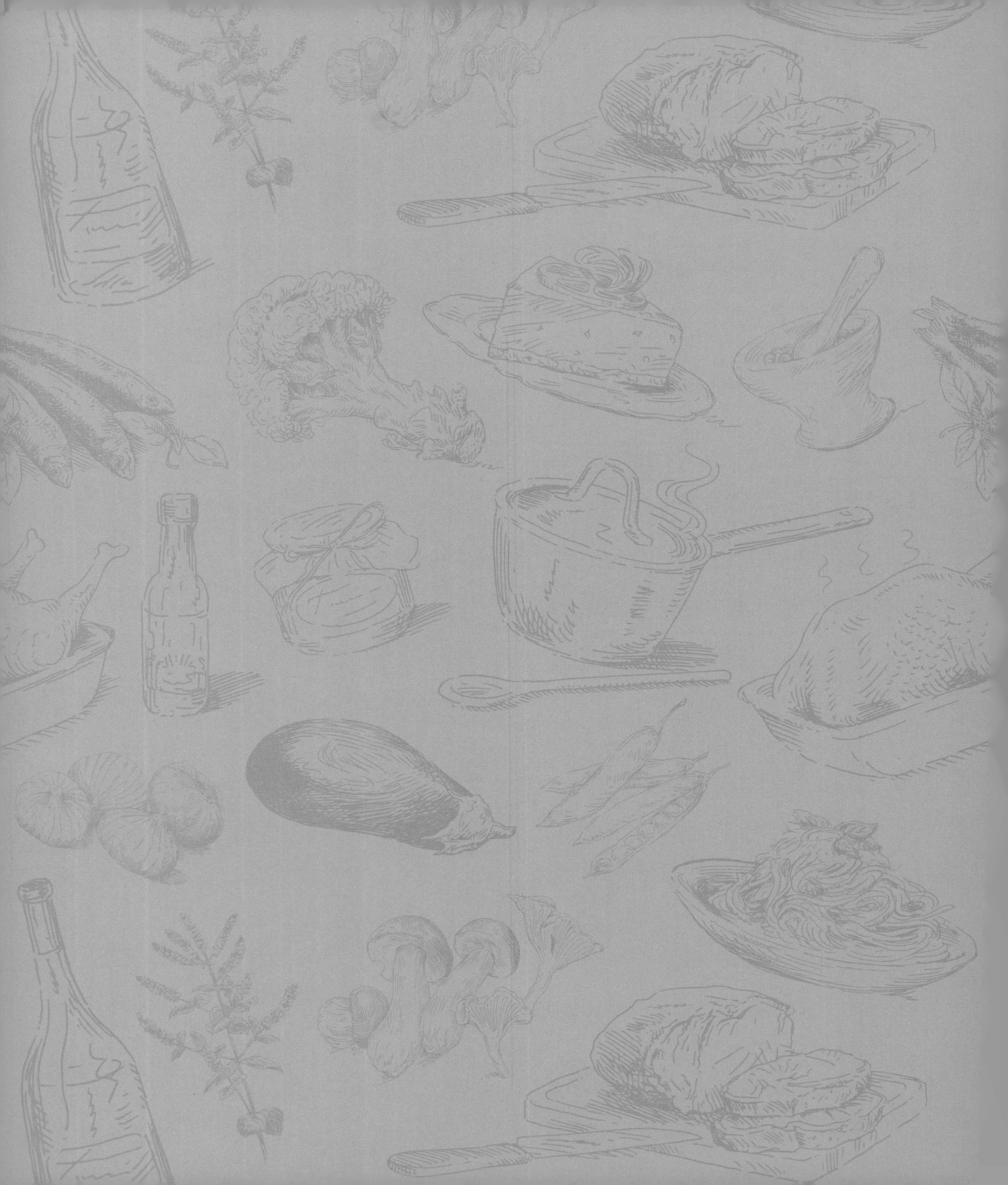

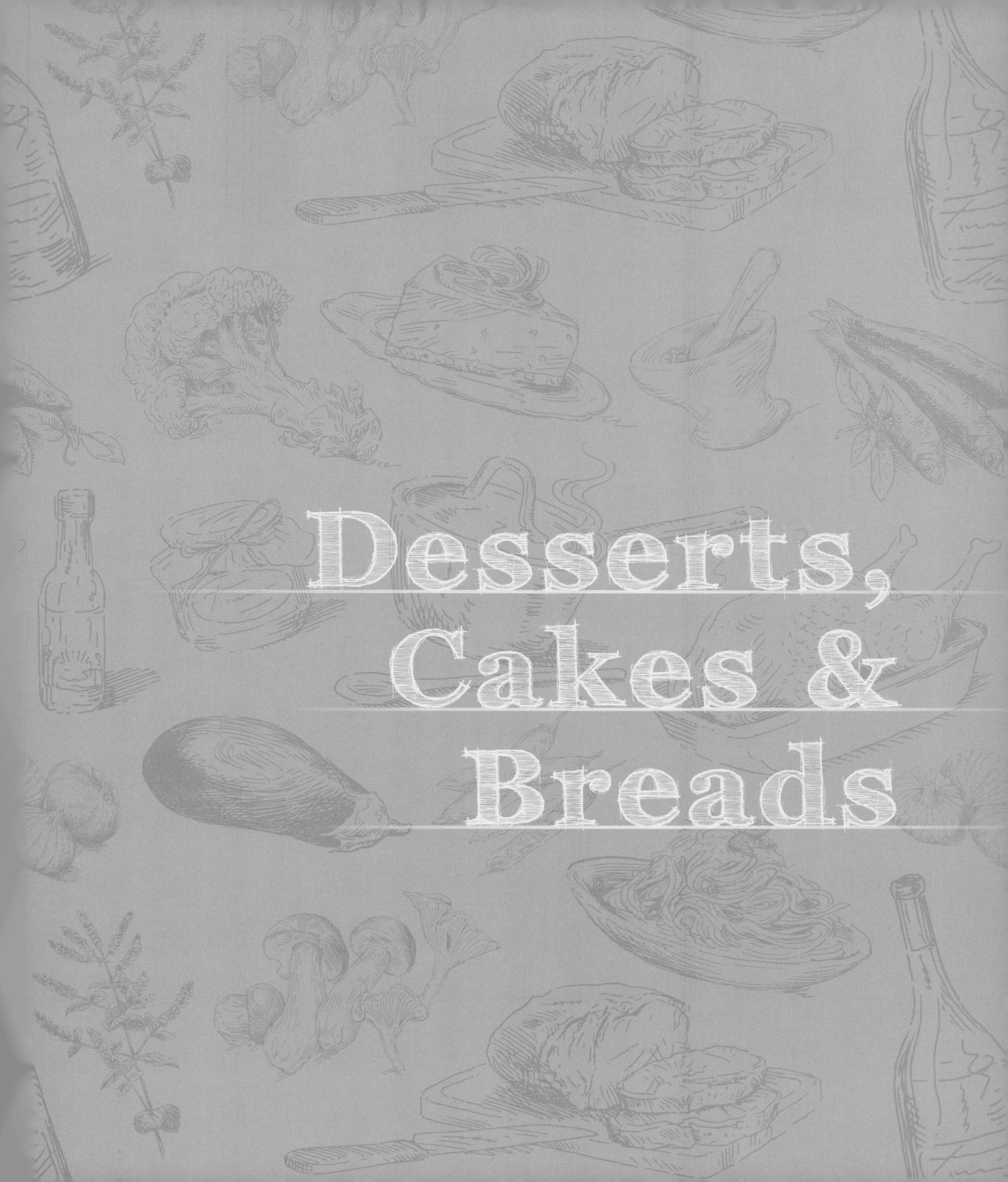

Desserts, Cakes & Breads

Fruit & nut-studded amaranth pudding

PREPARATION 15 minutes   COOKING 35 minutes   SERVES 4

- 3 cups (750 ml) low-fat milk
- 1 cup (250 g) wholegrain amaranth
- 1/4 cup (45 g) rapadura sugar, soft brown sugar or maple sugar
- 2 teaspoons finely grated orange zest, plus extra for garnish
- 2 teaspoons finely grated lemon zest, plus extra for garnish
- 1/4 teaspoon ground cardamom
- 2 tablespoons pine nuts, toasted
- 1/3 cup (40 g) raisins, plus extra for garnish
- 1/2 teaspoon natural vanilla extract

Each serving provides
1524 kJ, 364 kcal, 14 g protein, 6 g fat (<1 g saturated fat), 62 g carbohydrate (27 g sugars), 3 g fibre, 126 mg sodium

Combine the milk, amaranth, sugar, orange zest, lemon zest and cardamom in a large saucepan and bring to the boil. Reduce the heat to low, cover and simmer for 35 minutes, stirring occasionally, or until the amaranth is tender.

Remove from the heat and stir in the pine nuts, raisins and vanilla. Spoon the pudding into serving bowls or glasses, top with zest and raisins. Serve the pudding at room temperature or refrigerate if you prefer and serve chilled.

Fibre fact

The importance of fibre, particularly in special diets, has encouraged the search for new sources of fibre-rich foods. Amaranth is a very good nutrient alternative and has even more fibre content than quinoa. Most major supermarkets now stock amaranth and you'll also find it in health-food stores. Cultivated since ancient times, amaranth is rich in magnesium, iron, fibre, and the amino acid lysine (which is rare in plant sources). In this homey pudding, the amaranth remains crunchy and has a nutty flavour, which is emphasised by the addition of pine nuts.

Apricot hazelnut meringue cake

PREPARATION 30 minutes, plus 1 hour chilling   COOKING 1 hour   SERVES 8

$1^1/2$ cups (270 g) dried apricots
$1^1/2$ cups (375 ml) boiling water
4 eggwhites
1 teaspoon white vinegar
a pinch of salt
1 cup (220 g) caster (superfine) sugar
$^3/4$ cup (80 g) ground hazelnuts
300 ml (10 fl oz) pouring (light) cream, whipped and chilled
4 fresh apricots, stones removed and thinly sliced, to serve
3 cups (400 g) blackberries, to serve

Each serving provides
1504 kJ, 359 kcal, 7 g protein, 14 g fat (5 g saturated fat), 50 g carbohydrate (49 g sugars), 8 g fibre, 53 mg sodium

Preheat the oven to 120°C (250°F/Gas $^1/4$–$^1/2$). Line two large baking trays with baking (parchment) paper.

Place the dried apricots in a heatproof bowl and pour the boiling water over to cover. Leave to soak for at least 20 minutes to soften.

Beat the eggwhites in a large bowl with the vinegar and salt until soft peaks start to form, then continue beating while gradually adding the sugar, until the sugar has dissolved and the mixture is glossy, thick and heavy. Fold in the ground hazelnuts to combine.

With a spatula or palette knife, spread the hazelnut mixture onto the baking paper to make four identical shapes about 5 mm ($^1/4$ inch) thick (rectangles or rounds work equally well). Bake for 1 hour, swapping the trays halfway through to ensure even cooking – when done, the meringue shapes should be crisp and dry, and the undersides should not be sticky. Remove from the oven and allow to cool completely.

Meanwhile, use a blender or food processor to purée the soaked dried apricots with about $^1/2$ cup (125 ml) of their soaking water (you may need a little more to achieve a smooth paste).

Place a meringue shape on a serving plate and spread with a thin layer of apricot paste. Spread a dollop of whipped cream over the top and add another meringue layer. Repeat to make another layer and then top with the remaining apricot and cream. Refrigerate for 1 hour.

To serve, decorate the meringue with the apricot slices and fresh blackberries.

Fibre fact

This version of the classic pavlova adds hazelnuts and a fruit purée, providing lots more fibre than the traditional version. To make a cake that is very low in fat, try using whipped low-fat ricotta or quark instead of the whipped cream.

Orange & rockmelon sorbet

PREPARATION 15 minutes, plus 2–3 hours freezing *COOKING nil* *SERVES 4*

4 cups (600 g) rockmelon (cantaloupe) cubes
3/4 cup (180 ml) buttermilk
1/3 cup (115 g) maple syrup
1/4 cup (60 ml) orange juice
1/3 cup (75 g) sugar
1 teaspoon finely grated orange zest

Each serving provides
921 kJ, 220 kcal, 3 g protein, 1 g fat (<1 g saturated fat), 50 g carbohydrate (48 g sugars), 2 g fibre, 47 mg sodium

Put the rockmelon in a food processor and process to make a smooth purée. Transfer to a bowl and add the buttermilk, maple syrup, orange juice, sugar and orange zest, stirring well to combine.

Place in an ice cream machine and freeze according to the manufacturer's instructions. Alternatively, place in a large shallow dish and freeze for 2–3 hours, or until almost frozen. Remove from the freezer and cut into chunks, then process in a food processor until smooth. If not serving straight away, re-freeze the sorbet until needed, but allow it to soften in the refrigerator for 30 minutes before serving.

Fibre fact

Rockmelon (cantaloupe) is an excellent source of vitamins A, B_6 and C, as well as fibre, folate, potassium and niacin. Oranges are high in vitamin C and natural fibre and a host of other nutrients. Combining these two fruits makes a healthy, refreshing dessert.

Baked apples with sultanas & brandy

PREPARATION 15 minutes   COOKING 1 hour   SERVES 4

4 green apples
$2^1/_2$ tablespoons butter, at room temperature
$^1/_4$ cup (30 g) sultanas (golden raisins)
$^1/_4$ cup (30 g) raisins
2 teaspoons mixed (pumpkin pie) spice
1 tablespoon julienned orange zest, plus extra, to garnish
$^1/_3$ cup (80 ml) orange juice
$^1/_4$ cup (45 g) soft brown sugar
$^1/_3$ cup (80 ml) brandy

Preheat the oven to 180°C (350°F/Gas 4). Core the apples, score a cross in the top of each and then make a slit in the skin around the centre of each one with a small knife.

Combine the butter, sultanas, raisins, mixed spice and orange zest in a mixing bowl. Stuff the core of each apple with this mixture. Arrange in a large baking dish, then sprinkle over the orange juice and sugar.

Pour $^2/_3$ cup (150 ml) water into the dish with the apples, then pour 1 tablespoon brandy over each apple. Bake in the oven for 45–60 minutes, or until the apples are soft and the sugar has caramelised. Pour a little of the cooking liquid over each apple, garnish with a little extra orange zest and serve immediately.

Each serving provides
1240 kJ, 296 kcal, 1 g protein, 10 g fat (6 g saturated fat), 42 g carbohydrate (40 g sugars), 4 g fibre, 99 mg sodium

Fibre fact

Apples with their skin on are a rich source of dietary fibre. One medium apple contains more than $3^1/_2$ g fibre.

Blackberry fool

PREPARATION 5 minutes, plus 30 minutes chilling   COOKING nil   SERVES 4

- 2 cups (260 g) blackberries, plus extra, to garnish
- 1/2 cup (110 g) caster (superfine) sugar
- 1/2 cup (125 g) low-fat sour cream
- 1 cup (250 ml) low-fat evaporated milk, chilled
- almond bread, to serve (optional)

Each serving provides
1019 kJ, 243 kcal, 7 g protein, 5 g fat (3 g saturated fat), 41 g carbohydrate (41 g sugars), 4 g fibre, 77 mg sodium

Put the blackberries and sugar in a food processor and process to make a smooth purée. Stir in the sour cream.

Whip the evaporated milk in a mixing bowl until stiff peaks form. Fold the whipped milk into the blackberry purée and divide among serving dishes. Refrigerate for at least 30 minutes.

To serve, decorate the top of each fool with extra blackberries, and serve with slices of almond bread on the side, if desired.

Fibre fact

Because of their many tiny seeds, blackberries contain 8 g of fibre in a single cup. These luscious berries are loaded with pectin, a type of fibre that can help lower cholesterol; they also contain health-boosting carotenoids. Frozen fruit contains just as much fibre as raw fruit.

Kiwi fruit & blueberry salad

PREPARATION 15 minutes   COOKING 2 minutes   SERVES 4

Put the port and lemon zest in a saucepan and bring to the boil. Add the kiwi fruit, then reduce the heat to low and poach the fruit for 1–2 minutes. Remove the pan from the heat, then use a slotted spoon to remove the fruit to a plate, discarding the lemon peel. Allow to cool, then arrange the kiwi fruit on serving plates with the blueberries.

To make the raspberry cream, place the raspberries in a fine sieve over a bowl. Press the berries with the back of a spoon to make a fine purée without any seeds. Reserve a little purée for decoration. Stir the icing sugar, vanilla sugar and raspberry liqueur into the raspberry purée, then fold in the cream until well combined.

Dust the kiwi fruit and blueberries with icing sugar. Scatter over the toasted almonds and spoon a little raspberry cream onto each plate. Using a teaspoon, swirl in a little of the reserved purée before serving.

Fibre fact

Also called Chinese gooseberry, kiwi fruit makes a pretty addition to any fruit-based dessert. It can be served with the skin on – simply rub it gently with a clean tea towel (dish cloth) to remove the loose 'hairs' before slicing. Eaten this way, kiwi fruit is one of the highest-fibre fruits.

1/2 cup (125 ml) port or red wine
a few small strips lemon zest
8 kiwi fruit, peeled and sliced crosswise
250 g (8 oz) blueberries
icing (confectioners') sugar, to serve
1/2 cup (60 g) slivered almonds, toasted, to serve

Raspberry cream

150 g (5 oz) frozen raspberries, thawed
2/3 cup (80 g) icing (confectioners') sugar
2 teaspoons vanilla sugar
2 tablespoons raspberry liqueur or almond liqueur
1/2 cup (125 g) thick (heavy/double) cream or low-fat Greek-style yogurt

Each serving provides
1669 kJ, 399 kcal, 9 g protein, 9 g fat (1 g saturated fat), 57 g carbohydrate (50 g sugars), 10 g fibre, 62 mg sodium

Pineapple salad with almond brittle

PREPARATION 40 minutes   COOKING 10 minutes   SERVES 4

canola oil, for brushing
1/4 cup (55 g) caster (superfine) sugar
1 teaspoon lemon juice
1–2 teaspoons ground cinnamon
1 cup (125 g) slivered almonds
2 kg (4 lb) pineapple, peeled and thinly sliced into rounds
2 tablespoons soft brown sugar
orange zest, to garnish

Yogurt cream

1/2 cup (125 g) natural (plain) yogurt
2–3 tablespoons orange juice
1/2 teaspoon finely grated orange zest
1 tablespoon orange liqueur
1 teaspoon icing (confectioners') sugar
1/2 cup (125 g) whipping cream

Each serving provides
2711 kJ, 648 kcal, 14 g protein, 34 g fat (11 g saturated fat), 69 g carbohydrate (67 g sugars), 14 g fibre, 51 mg sodium

To make the almond brittle, brush a little canola oil over a piece of baking (parchment) paper; set aside. Put the caster sugar, lemon juice and 1/4 cup (60 ml) water in a heavy-based saucepan with a heatproof handle; cook over medium heat until the sugar caramelises. Remove from the heat and quickly stir in the cinnamon and slivered almonds to combine. Spread the mixture onto the prepared baking paper, keeping the almond slivers as far apart as possible. Allow to cool, then chop into pieces.

Preheat the oven to 220°C (425°F/Gas 7). Arrange the pineapple slices on ovenproof plates and sprinkle the brown sugar over the top. Bake for about 8–10 minutes. Allow to cool to lukewarm.

Meanwhile, make the yogurt cream. Combine the yogurt, orange juice, orange zest, orange liqueur and icing sugar in a bowl until smooth and creamy. Whip the cream until stiff peaks form and fold into the yogurt mixture.

To serve, spoon the yogurt cream over the pineapple on each plate and sprinkle the almond brittle over the top. Garnish with orange zest and serve lukewarm.

Fibre fact

Pineapples are loaded with vitamins, minerals and fibre.

Caramelised orange compote

PREPARATION 15 minutes COOKING 2 minutes SERVES 4

Preheat the grill (broiler). Peel the oranges and cut each orange into skinless segments, making sure all the white pith has been removed.

Place the orange segments in a shallow gratin dish or baking dish and sprinkle the combined sugar and cinnamon over the top. Scatter over the orange zest, then grill (broil) for 2 minutes, or until the sugar melts.

Fibre fact

You will get much more fibre from eating the flesh than from drinking the juice of oranges. Oranges are outstanding sources of vitamin C; they also supply folate and flavonoids as well as fibre. Choose sweet varieties for this lovely dessert.

4 oranges
1/4 cup (45 g) soft brown sugar
1/2 teaspoon ground cinnamon
1 tablespoon julienned orange zest

Each serving provides
393 kJ, 94 kcal, 2 g protein, 1 g fat (0 g saturated fat), 22 g carbohydrate (22 g sugars), 3 g fibre, 6 mg sodium

Fruity steamed Christmas pudding

PREPARATION 40 minutes   COOKING 4½ hours   SERVES 10

2/3 cup (100 g) dried currants
2/3 cup (85 g) raisins
2/3 cup (85 g) sultanas (golden raisins)
1/2 cup (90 g) dried pitted dates, chopped
1/2 cup (75 g) dried apricots, chopped
2/3 cup (80 g) dried cranberries
grated zest and juice of 1 large orange
1/4 cup (60 ml) sherry or brandy
125 g (4 oz) salt-reduced margarine
1/2 cup (115 g) firmly packed dark brown sugar
2 eggs, beaten
1 apple, peeled, cored and diced
1 large carrot, finely grated
1/3 cup (30 g) flaked almonds, toasted
1/2 cup (75 g) self-raising flour
2 teaspoons mixed spice (pumpkin pie) spice
1 1/4 cups (100 g) fresh white breadcrumbs

Brandy sauce

1/3 cup (40 g) cornflour (cornstarch)
3 1/2 cups (875 ml) low-fat milk
1/4 cup (55 g) caster (superfine) sugar, or to taste
1/4 cup (60 ml) brandy

Each serving provides
2020 kJ, 483 kcal, 9 g protein, 15 g fat (3 g saturated fat), 76 g carbohydrate (59 g sugars), 5 g fibre, 257 mg sodium

Place all the dried fruit in a bowl. Add the orange zest and juice, and the sherry or brandy, stir to combine, then set aside to soak.

Lightly grease a 5 cup (1.25 litre) pudding basin (mould) and line the base with baking (parchment) paper.

Beat together the margarine and brown sugar with an electric mixer until light and fluffy, then gradually add the eggs and beat until well combined. Stir in the apple, carrot, almonds and soaked fruits. Sift in the flour and mixed spice, add the breadcrumbs and mix well until well combined.

Spoon the mixture into the pudding basin and smooth the top. Lay a doubled sheet of baking paper over the top, and then a layer of foil. Fold to make a pleat in the centre, then smooth down over the basin and tie securely with kitchen string.

Bring a deep saucepan of water to the boil. Place the basin inside the pan and steam for 3 hours, making sure that you keep topping up the pan with water as required.

Remove the basin and take off the foil and paper. Cover with a tea towel (dish cloth) and cool completely. Wrap in fresh baking paper and then foil and store in a cool, dark place for up to 3 months. On the day of serving, steam the pudding for a further 1 1/2 hours.

To make the brandy sauce, blend the cornflour with 1/3 cup (80 ml) of the milk. Heat the remaining milk in a saucepan until almost boiling, then pour over the cornflour mixture, stirring well. Return to the pan and stir over medium heat until thickened. Simmer for a further 1–2 minutes, stirring continuously, then add the sugar and brandy and stir to dissolve. Taste for sweetness, adding a little more sugar if needed.

Turn the pudding onto a serving plate and serve with the hot brandy sauce on the side.

Fibre fact

Lighter than a traditional festive pudding, this version is packed full of fruit and therefore lots of fibre goodness.

Summer pudding

PREPARATION 25 minutes, plus 8 hours chilling   COOKING 2 minutes   SERVES 8

2 cups (260 g) blackberries
2 cups (250 g) raspberries
1 cup (155 g) blueberries
1/2 cup (160 g) seedless raspberry jam
1/2 cup (110 g) caster (superfine) sugar
3 teaspoons lemon juice
10 slices firm-textured high-fibre white sandwich bread (preferably a little stale)
whipped cream, to serve

Each serving provides
907 kJ, 217 kcal, 4 g protein, 1 g fat (0 g saturated fat), 47 g carbohydrate (34 g sugars), 6 g fibre, 154 mg sodium

Combine the blackberries, raspberries, blueberries, jam and sugar in a saucepan over medium–low heat. Bring to a simmer and cook for 1 minute, then stir in the lemon juice to combine. Remove from the heat and set aside to cool.

Line a 5 cup (1.25 litre) pudding basin (mould) or large mixing bowl with plastic wrap, leaving a 13 cm (5 inch) overhang over the side – this will later be used to cover the pudding.

Remove the crusts from the bread. Slice the bread in half on the diagonal and arrange the triangular slices on the bottom and sides of the dish, overlapping slightly – there should be bread slices left over for the top.

Spoon the berries and juices into the basin. Cover with the remaining bread, trimming all sides. Cover with plastic wrap and fold the overhang over the top. Place a weight on top, such as a heavy can, and refrigerate for at least 8 hours.

When you are ready to serve, turning the pudding out onto a serving plate, removing the plastic. Cut the pudding into wedges and serve with whipped cream, if desired.

Fibre fact

The luscious berries in this recipe are loaded with pectin, a type of fibre that can help lower cholesterol.

Sweet & spicy carrot pie with nut crust

PREPARATION 20 minutes   COOKING 1 hour   SERVES 8

1/2 cup (50 g) walnuts, toasted
1/2 cup (70 g) hazelnuts, toasted
1 cup (125 g) sweet wheat biscuit crumbs (graham crackers)
1/4 cup (55 g) soft brown sugar
1 1/4 teaspoons ground cinnamon
1 1/4 teaspoons ground ginger
3 tablespoons canola oil or light olive oil
2 tablespoons butter, melted
500 g (1 lb) carrots, peeled and chopped
1 cup (220 g) sugar
1 tablespoon plain (all-purpose) flour
1/4 teaspoon ground nutmeg
a pinch of cloves
4 large eggs, lightly beaten
3/4 cup (185 ml) low-fat milk

Each serving provides
2018 kJ, 482 kcal, 10 g protein, 27 g fat (6 g saturated fat), 60 g carbohydrate (44 g sugars), 4 g fibre, 194 mg sodium

To make the nut crust, put the walnuts and hazelnuts in a food processor and process until coarsely chopped. Add the biscuit crumbs, brown sugar, 1/4 teaspoon of the cinnamon and 1/4 teaspoon of the ground ginger. Process to combine, then add the canola oil and melted butter and process until the crumbs are moist. Press the crumb mixture into 23 cm (9 inch) round, deep pie dish, line the base and side in an even layer.

Cook the carrots in a large saucepan of boiling water for about 20 minutes, or until tender. Drain well, then transfer to a food processor and process to make a smooth purée.

Preheat the oven to 200°C (400°F/Gas 6). Put the sugar, flour, nutmeg, cloves and the remaining ginger and cinnamon into a bowl and stir to combine. Add to the carrot purée and process to combine. Add the eggs and milk; process until smooth and well blended. Pour the carrot mixture over the pie crust.

Bake in the oven for about 40 minutes, or until a skewer inserted into the centre of the pie comes out clean. Cut into slices and serve warm or at room temperature. If you prefer you can refrigerate the pie for several hours and serve chilled.

Fibre fact

Most pie crusts are very low in fibre. The nuts in this crust make it much more nutritious and high in fibre. You can boost the fibre further by choosing sweet wholemeal (whole-wheat) biscuits for the crumbs.

Carrot & brazil nut cake

PREPARATION 30 minutes, plus cooling COOKING 50 minutes SERVES 12

$1^1/_2$ cups (225 g) self-raising wholemeal (whole-wheat) flour

$1^1/_2$ cups (225 g) self-raising flour

1 teaspoon ground cinnamon

$^2/_3$ cups (100 g) brazil nuts or cashew or macadamia nuts

$^1/_2$ cup (60 g) raisins

$^2/_3$ cup (155 g) soft brown sugar

$^3/_4$ cup (180 ml) canola oil

4 eggs

200 g (7 oz) carrots, peeled and finely grated

finely grated zest and juice of $^1/_2$ orange

Orange ricotta icing (frosting)

1 cup (250 g) low-fat ricotta

$^1/_4$ cup (30 g) icing (confectioners') sugar, sifted

finely grated zest of $^1/_2$ orange

Each serving provides
1798 kJ, 430 kcal, 10 g protein, 24 g fat (4 g saturated fat), 45 g carbohydrate (21 g sugars), 4 g fibre, 329 mg sodium

Preheat the oven to 180°C (350°F/Gas 4). Lightly grease a 20 cm (8 inch) round spring-form cake tin and line the base with baking (parchment) paper.

Sift both the flours and the cinnamon into a large bowl, tipping in any bran left in the sieve. Coarsely chop about two-thirds of the brazil nuts; stir into the flour with the raisins. Thinly slice the remaining nuts lengthwise and set aside to use for decorating the cake.

In another bowl, use a wooden spoon to beat together the sugar and canola oil until well combined. Beat in the eggs, one at a time, making sure each is well incorporated before adding the next. Stir in the grated carrots, orange zest and juice. Using a large metal spoon, fold the carrot mixture into the flour mixture, only until just combined – do not overmix.

Spoon the mixture into the prepared tin and bake for 50 minutes, or until the cake has risen and is firm to the touch. Leave the cake in the tin for 5 minutes, then remove from the tin and cool completely on a wire rack.

To make the orange ricotta icing (frosting), beat together the ricotta, sugar and orange zest in a bowl. Spread the icing over the cooled cake and scatter the reserved sliced nuts over the top. Cut into slices and serve.

Fibre fact

Because of their fibre content, carrots are filling and will leave you feeling satisfied for longer. Most vegetables are more nutritious eaten raw, but carrots have more to offer when cooked. This is because cooking breaks down the tough cell membranes in the carrots, and makes it easier for the body to absorb the anti-oxidant beta-carotene. The wholemeal (whole-wheat) flour in this cake provides good amounts of fibre.

Carrot & apricot muffins with pecans

PREPARATION 22 minutes   COOKING 30 minutes   MAKES 12 muffins

2 cups (300 g) plain (all-purpose) flour
1 3/4 teaspoons baking powder
3/4 teaspoon ground cinnamon
1/2 cup (135 g) unsweetened puréed cooked apple
1/4 cup (55 g) sugar
1/4 cup (45 g) soft brown sugar
2 tablespoons vegetable oil
1 egg
1 eggwhite
1/4 cup (25 g) pecans, toasted and chopped
2 cups (300 g) firmly packed grated carrots
1/3 cup (45 g) chopped dried apricots

Each muffin provides
776 kJ, 185 kcal, 4 g protein, 5 g fat (1 g saturated fat), 31 g carbohydrate (12 g sugars), 2 g fibre, 93 mg sodium

Preheat the oven to 190°C (375°F/Gas 5). Line a 12-hole muffin tin with paper muffin cases.

Combine the flour, baking powder and cinnamon in a mixing bowl. Combine the apple purée in a separate bowl with both of the sugars, the oil, egg and eggwhite, stirring well to combine. Fold through the pecans, carrots and apricots until just combined.

Make a well in the centre of the flour. Stir in the carrot mixture until just moistened. Spoon into the muffin cases and bake for 30 minutes, or until a skewer inserted in the centre of a muffin comes out clean. Allow to cool slightly on a wire rack before serving.

Fibre fact

Both apples and carrots are a good source of pectin, which is one of the soluble fibres that helps to lower cholesterol and slow the rise in blood glucose. You can increase the fibre in these muffins further by replacing half of the flour with wholemeal (whole-wheat) flour.

Carrot & pineapple cake

PREPARATION 20 minutes   COOKING 30 minutes   SERVES 16

Preheat the oven to 180°C (350°F/Gas 4). Lightly grease two 23 cm (9 inch) round cake tins.

Put the flour, cinnamon, baking powder and bicarbonate of soda in a mixing bowl and stir to combine.

In a separate bowl, combine the sugar, vegetable oil, eggs and apple purée. Add the flour mixture and stir until just combined, then add the carrots, the pineapple and its juice, and the raisins and walnuts. Mix everything together, then divide the mixture evenly between the prepared tins.

Bake in the oven for 45–50 minutes, or until a skewer inserted in the centre of each cake comes out clean. Leave to cool in the tins for 30 minutes, then turn each cake out onto a wire rack to cool completely.

To make the cream cheese icing (frosting), use electric beaters to beat the cream cheese in a large bowl on low speed for about 1 minute. Add the icing sugar and vanilla and beat until smooth and well combined.

Place one cake on a serving plate and spread over one-third of the icing. Place the second cake on top and spread over the remaining icing to cover the top and sides of the cakes. Cut into slices and serve.

Fibre fact

Pineapples and carrots are rich in fibre. This cake is also one of the sweetest ways to get your quota of vitamin A, with 80 per cent of the daily requirement contained in each slice.

2 1/2 cups (375 g) plain (all-purpose) flour

2 teaspoons ground cinnamon

1 teaspoon baking powder

1 1/2 teaspoons bicarbonate of soda (baking soda)

1 1/2 cups (330 g) sugar

1/2 cup (125 ml) vegetable oil

4 eggs

1/2 cup (135 g) unsweetened puréed cooked apple

3 1/3 cups (500 g) firmly packed grated carrots

250 g (8 oz) canned crushed pineapple in natural juice

1/2 cup (60 g) seedless raisins

1/2 cup (50 g) walnuts, chopped

Cream cheese icing (frosting)

1 cup (250 g) low-fat cream cheese, softened

5 cups (625 g) icing (confectioners') sugar, sifted

1 teaspoon natural vanilla extract

Each serving provides
1971 kJ, 471 kcal, 6 g protein, 14 g fat (3 g saturated fat), 84 g carbohydrate (65 g sugars), 3 g fibre, 252 mg sodium

Boiled fruit cake

PREPARATION 20 minutes   COOKING 2¼ hours   SERVES 12

5 cups (925 g) mixed dried fruit
2 cups (320 g) chopped pitted dates
1/2 cup (105 g) glacé cherries, chopped
125 g (4 oz) butter
1 cup (185 g) soft brown sugar
2 teaspoons mixed (pumpkin pie) spice
3/4 cup (180 ml) sherry, plus an extra 1/4 cup (60 ml), for drizzling
2 eggs
1/4 cup (80 g) apricot jam
1 cup (150 g) self-raising flour
1 cup (150 g) plain (all-purpose) flour
1/3 cup (50 g) blanched almonds

Each serving provides
2515 kJ, 601 kcal, 7 g protein, 13 g fat (6 g saturated fat), 113 g carbohydrate (94 g sugars), 9 g fibre, 2446 mg sodium

Preheat the oven to 160°C (320°F/Gas 2–3). Grease and line a 20 cm (8 inch) round cake tin with a double layer of baking (parchment) paper to ensure the cake won't cook too quickly.

Put the mixed fruit, dates, cherries, butter, sugar, mixed spice and sherry in a large saucepan over medium–low heat. Stir until the butter has melted and the mixture comes to the boil. Boil for 3 minutes, then remove from the heat and leave to cool.

Add the eggs and jam to the fruit mixture, stirring well, then sift in the flours and use a large metal spoon to combine. Spoon into the cake tin and sprinkle over the almonds.

Bake for 2 hours, or until a skewer inserted into the centre of the cake has no raw mixture on it (the skewer will not be entirely clean). Pour the extra sherry onto the hot cake, then wrap the cake in a clean tea towel (dish cloth) and leave to cool. When the cake is cold, remove the tea towel, then wrap the cake in baking paper or foil and store in an airtight container.

Fibre fact

Dried fruit has a low glycaemic index thanks to its high fibre content. You can increase the fibre further by replacing half of the flour with wholemeal (whole-wheat) flour.

Raspberry & walnut cake

PREPARATION 30 minutes   COOKING 50 minutes   SERVES 8

Preheat the oven to 180°C (350°F/Gas 4). Lightly grease a 20 cm (8 inch) square baking tin and line the base and sides with baking (parchment) paper.

Put the flour, sugar, cinnamon and baking powder in a large bowl and stir to combine. In a separate bowl, mix together the milk, egg, butter and oil, then add to the dry ingredients. Fold through the walnuts and lemon zest to combine.

Pour the mixture into the prepared tin and scatter over the raspberries. Bake in the oven for 50 minutes, or until a skewer inserted into the centre of the cake comes out clean. Leave to cool in the tin for 10 minutes before turning out onto a wire rack to cool completely. Cut into slices and serve.

Fibre fact

Wholemeal (whole-wheat) flour is heavier than white, so often requires extra liquid in the recipe. Take care not to stir the mixture too much or it can become tough. The walnuts help to keep the texture of this cake light, as well as adding extra fibre.

- 2 1/2 cups (375 g) plain wholemeal (whole-wheat) flour
- 3/4 cup (165 g) firmly packed light brown sugar
- 1 teaspoon ground cinnamon
- 1 tablespoon baking powder
- 1 cup (250 ml) low-fat milk
- 1 egg
- 60 g (2 oz) butter, melted
- 2 tablespoons vegetable oil
- 3/4 cup (75 g) walnuts, chopped
- 1 teaspoon finely grated lemon zest
- 2 cups (250 g) fresh raspberries

Each serving provides
1769 kJ, 423 kcal, 10 g protein, 19 g fat (6 g saturated fat), 53 g carbohydrate (21 g sugars), 8 g fibre, 159 mg sodium

Fruit & nut bread

PREPARATION 50 minutes, plus 3 hours rising   COOKING 30–40 minutes   SERVES 10

2 2/3 cups (400) strong white (bread) flour

grated zest of 1/2 lemon

2 teaspoons dry (powdered) yeast

1/2 cup (90 g) dried apricots, chopped

1/2 cup (90 g) chopped dried pears

1/3 cup (90 g) pitted prunes, chopped

1/3 cup (60 g) dried figs, chopped

1/3 cup (50 g) chopped mixed nuts, such as almonds, hazelnuts and cashews

Each serving (2 slices) provides
1013 kJ, 242 kcal, 7 g protein, 3 g fat (1 g saturated fat), 46 g carbohydrate (14 g sugars), 5 g fibre, 21 mg sodium

Put the flour, lemon zest and yeast in a large bowl. Add all of the chopped fruits and nuts and stir well to combine. Add 1 cup (250 ml) tepid water and use your hands to work the mixture into a soft, heavy dough.

Turn the dough out onto a lightly floured work surface and knead for 10 minutes, or until it is soft and elastic. Place the dough in a lightly greased bowl, cover with a damp tea towel (dish cloth) and set aside in a warm, draught-free place for 2 hours, or until doubled in size.

Knock back the dough then knead again on a lightly floured work surface until it returns to its original size. Shape into a ball, place on a lightly greased baking tray and cover with a damp tea towel. Set aside again, for about 1 hour, or until doubled in size.

Preheat the oven to 200°C (400°F/Gas 6). Bake the loaf for 30–40 minutes, or until it is nicely browned and sounds hollow when tapped on the base. Cover with foil during cooking if it is becoming too brown. Transfer to a wire rack and leave to cool. This bread can be kept for up to 5 days.

Fibre fact

This heavily fruited German-style loaf contains no added fat (the fat present comes from the nuts), but the fibre-rich dried fruits – a mixture of apricots, pears, prunes and figs – give it a rich, moist texture and good storing qualities.

Toasted oat & bran tea bread

PREPARATION 15 minutes   COOKING 1½ hours   MAKES 12 slices

- 1 1/2 cups (150 g) rolled (porridge) oats
- 1/2 cup (45 g) linseeds (flax seeds)
- 1/2 cup (45 g) wheat bran
- 1 cup (150 g) plain (all-purpose) flour
- 1/2 cup (115 g) firmly packed soft brown sugar
- 2 teaspoons baking powder
- 1 1/4 cups (310 g) low-fat natural (plain) yogurt
- 2/3 cup (235 g) honey
- 1 large egg
- 1 cup (125 g) raisins

Preheat the oven to 180°C (350°F/Gas 4). Lightly grease a 23 x 13 cm (9 x 5 inch) loaf (bar) tin.

Place the oats, linseeds and wheat bran on a baking tray and bake for 7–9 minutes, or until the oats are golden brown. Transfer to a food processor and process until finely ground.

Transfer the oat mixture to a large bowl. Stir in the flour, brown sugar and baking powder.

In a separate bowl, whisk together the yogurt, honey, and egg. Make a well in the centre of the dry ingredients and fold in the yogurt mixture until just combined. Fold in the raisins.

Spoon the batter into the prepared tin, smoothing the top. Bake for 1 hour 20 minutes, or until a skewer inserted into the centre of the loaf comes out clean. Cool for 5 minutes in the tin, then turn the loaf out onto a wire rack to cool completely.

Each slice provides
1173 kJ, 280 kcal, 7 g protein, 4 g fat (1 g saturated fat), 55 g carbohydrate (35 g sugars), 5 g fibre, 158 mg sodium

Fibre fact

Linseeds, also known as flax seeds, are high in fibre and add a nutty flavour to this tea bread. Look for them in health-food stores, but do not buy pre-ground linseed meal, which loses much of its nutrient value due to exposure to air and light.
If you cannot easily find whole linseeds, use unhulled sesame seeds instead.

Quick wholemeal bread

PREPARATION 10 minutes, plus 30 minutes rising   COOKING 40 minutes   MAKES 14 slices

3 cups (450 g) plain wholemeal (whole-wheat) flour

2 teaspoons dry (powdered) yeast

1 teaspoon brown sugar or honey

1 tablespoon plain (all-purpose) flour, to dust

Each slice provides

449 kJ, 107 kcal, 4 g protein, 1 g fat (0 g saturated fat), 21 g carbohydrate (1 g sugars), 4 g fibre, 3 mg sodium

Lightly grease a 23 x 13 cm (9 x 5 inch) loaf (bar) tin and line the base and side with baking (parchment) paper.

Sift the flour into a large mixing bowl, tipping in any bran left in the sieve. Stir in the yeast and make a well in the centre.

Combine the sugar or honey with 450 ml (15 fl oz) tepid water, then pour into the dry ingredients. Beat vigorously with a wooden spoon for about 2 minutes, or until the dough comes away from the side of the bowl – it will be very soft and sticky.

Place the dough into the prepared tin, cover with a damp tea towel (dish cloth) and set aside in a warm, draught-free place for about 30 minutes, or until the dough has risen almost to the top of the tin.

Preheat the oven to 200°C (400°F/Gas 6). Dust the top of the loaf evenly with the plain flour and bake in the oven for 30–40 minutes, or until well risen and brown – when done, the loaf should feel light and sound hollow when tapped on the base.

Cool for 5 minutes in the tin, then turn the loaf out onto a wire rack to cool completely. This bread can be kept for up to 5 days.

Fibre fact

Full of fibre, this bread is based on the famous 'Grant loaf', invented in the 1940s by Doris Grant. With its dense, moist texture, it is a filling bread that makes excellent toast. With only one rising and no kneading, it couldn't be simpler to make.

Multigrain seeded loaf

PREPARATION 25 minutes, plus 2 hours rising   COOKING 35 minutes   SERVES 8

2 cups (300 g) strong white (bread) flour

1$^1/_3$ cups (200 g) strong wholemeal (whole-wheat) bread flour

$^3/_4$ cup (100 g) buckwheat flour

$^1/_2$ cup (95 g) coarse polenta (cornmeal)

2 teaspoons dry (powdered) yeast

1 teaspoon soft brown sugar

3 tablespoons sunflower seeds

2 tablespoons pumpkin seeds

2 tablespoons linseeds (flax seeds)

2 tablespoons sunflower oil

low-fat milk, to glaze

Each serving provides
1637 kJ, 391 kcal, 12 g protein, 11 g fat (1 g saturated fat), 62 g carbohydrate (2 g sugars), 8 g fibre, 10 mg sodium

Sift the white, wholemeal and buckwheat flours into a large bowl, tipping in any bran left in the sieve. Stir in the polenta, yeast and sugar.

Mix together the sunflower seeds, pumpkin seeds and linseeds, reserving 1 tablespoon to use for the topping. Stir the rest into the flour mixture.

Make a well in the dry ingredients and pour in the oil and 450 ml (15 fl oz) tepid water. Work the dry ingredients into the liquid to make a soft dough, adding water if the dough is too dry. Turn out onto a lightly floured work surface and knead for 10 minutes, or until smooth and elastic. Place in a large, lightly oiled bowl and cover with a damp tea towel (dish cloth). Set aside in a warm, draught-free place for 1$^1/_2$ hours, or until doubled in size.

Knock back the dough and knead firmly for a few minutes. Shape into a 20 cm (8 inch) round and place on a lightly greased baking tray. Cover with oiled plastic wrap and leave for 20–30 minutes, or until well risen and springy to the touch.

Preheat the oven to 230°C (450°F/Gas 8). Use a sharp knife to make slashes in the top of the loaf to mark 8 wedges. Brush the top with a little milk and sprinkle with the reserved mixed seeds.

Bake in the oven for 15 minutes, then reduce the oven temperature to 200°C (400°F/Gas 6). Bake for a further 15–20 minutes, or until the loaf is golden brown and sounds hollow when tapped on the base. Cool for 5 minutes in the tin, then turn the loaf out onto a wire rack to cool completely. This bread is best eaten on the day it is made.

Fibre fact

The mix of seeds in this high-fibre, nutty-textured loaf can be varied to your own taste, or you can use just one kind.

Index

A

adzuki beans, 14
almonds
  Bircher muesli, 18
  Crunchy toasted cereal with fruit & nuts, 26
  Fresh fruit muesli, 25
  Fruity steamed Christmas pudding, 228
  Kiwi fruit & blueberry salad, 225
  Pineapple salad with almond brittle, 226
amaranth pudding, Fruit & nut-studded, 214
apples
  Baked apples with sultanas & brandy, 221
  Bircher muesli, 18
  Carrot & apricot muffins with pecans, 236
  Carrot & pineapple cake, 239
  Cinnamon French toast with sautéed apples, 35
  Crab & avocado salad, 147
  Crunchy toasted cereal with fruit & nuts, 26
  Fresh fruit muesli, 25
  Fruity steamed Christmas pudding, 228
  Spiced cream of pumpkin soup, 44
  Winter fresh fruit salad, 22
apricots, dried
  Apricot hazelnut meringue cake, 217
  Baked couscous tomatoes, 181
  Braised root vegetables with dried apricots, 188
  Carrot & apricot muffins with pecans, 236
  Carrot & pineapple cake, 239
  Dried fruit, 211
  Fresh fruit muesli, 25
  Fruit & nut bread, 242
  Fruity steamed Christmas pudding, 228
  Moroccan braised chicken, 106
  Vegetarian pilaf, 76
artichokes
  Artichokes with lentils & beans, 111
  Spaghetti with artichokes & broad beans, 62
asparagus, Pasta with roasted, 65
avocado
  Crab & avocado salad, 147
  Mexican chicken salad with salsa, 143

B

Baba ganoush, 202
Banana cinnamon muffins, 28
barley, 12
  Barley & vegetable salad, 184
  Spiced barley & corn, 187
bean sprouts
  Crab & avocado salad, 147
beans, 14–15
  Mixed bean chilli soup, 57
  see also black beans; borlotti beans; broad beans, butterbeans; cannellini beans; green beans; kidney beans; lima beans, baby; soybeans
beef
  Beef & chickpea tagine, 89
  Beef niçoise salad, 132
  Beefy pasta salad, 135
  Chilli con carne with cornbread, 90
  New England simmered beef, 86
  Thai-style beef sandwich with coleslaw, 80
beetroot
  Beetroot and onion relish, 86
  Roasted potatoes & root vegetables, 177
  Russian bean salad, 156
berries
  Bircher muesli, 18
  see also blackberries; blueberries; raspberries
Bircher muesli, 18
black beans, 14
  Chilli bean & polenta bake, 126
black-eyed beans, 14
black-eyed peas
  Bean & rice salad, 162
  Caribbean vegetable stew, 115
blackberries
  Apricot hazelnut meringue cake, 217
  Blackberry fool, 222
  Summer pudding, 231
blackcurrants, 194
blue cheese
  Red lentil and celery soup, 47
  Roquefort & pear salad, 170
blueberries
  Breakfast bread pudding with berries, 29
  Kiwi fruit & blueberry salad, 225
  Porridge with summer fruits, 32
  Summer pudding, 231
Boiled fruit cake, 240
borlotti beans, 14
  Mixed bean cassoulet, 119
  Spicy chicken tostadas, 70
  Tuscan-style baked polenta, 125
brandy, Baked apples with sultanas &, 221
Brandy sauce, 228
brazil nut cake, Carrot &, 235
bread
  Fruit & nut, 242
  Multigrain seeded loaf, 249
  Quick wholemeal, 246
  Toasted oat & bran tea, 245
bread pudding with berries, Breakfast, 29
broad beans, 14
  Beef niçoise salad, 132
  Mushroom and winter vegetable soup, 53
  Spaghetti with artichokes and broad beans, 62
broccoli
  Beefy pasta salad, 135
  Curried chicken and vegetables, 105
  see also Chinese broccoli
buckwheat, 12
burghul
  Burghul & fish salad with lemon dressing, 148
  Crab & avocado salad, 147
  Fresh fruit muesli, 25
  Tabouleh, 204
  Vegetarian pilaf, 76
burritos, Mexican bean, 73
butterbeans, 15
  Artichokes with lentils & beans, 111
  Lemony beans, 190
  Mediterranean chicken, 101
  Mixed bean cassoulet, 119
  Pork & bean chilli, 97
  Roasted vegetables & butterbeans, 178
  Vegetarian pilaf, 76
  White beans & silverbeet, 198

C

cabbage
  Brown rice & chickpea pilaf, 201
  Chicken & soba noodles, 58
  Crunchy nut coleslaw, 182
  Mushroom and winter vegetable soup, 53
  New England simmered beef, 86
  Stir-fried vegetable curry, 79
  Thai-style beef sandwich with coleslaw, 80
  see also red cabbage
cakes
  Apricot hazelnut meringue, 217
  Boiled fruit, 240
  Carrot & brazil nut, 235
  Carrot & pineapple, 239
  Raspberry & walnut, 241
cannellini beans, 15
  Mediterranean chicken, 101
  Pork & bean chilli, 97
  Speedy two-bean chilli, 118
  White bean garlic dip, 203
  White beans & silverbeet, 198
capsicum
  Mediterranean roasted vegetable soup, 50
  Mediterranean stuffed vegetables, 193
  Mexican bean burritos, 73
  Mixed bean chilli soup, 57
  Persian-style couscous with roast vegetables, 197
  Roasted capsicum, 122
  Seafood gumbo, 109
  Spicy chicken tostadas, 70
  Vegetable salad with tuna, 144
  Warm grilled mixed vegetable salad, 191
  White bean salad with sesame dressing, 149
Caramelised orange compote, 227
Caribbean vegetable stew, 115
carrots
  Braised root vegetables with dried apricots, 188
  Carrot & apricot muffins with pecans, 236
  Carrot & brazil nut cake, 235

Carrot & pineapple cake, 239
Chicken & soba noodles, 58
Curried chicken and vegetables, 105
Fruity Moroccan vegetable tagine, 112
Fruity steamed Christmas pudding, 228
New England simmered beef, 86
Red lentil and celery soup, 47
Roasted potatoes & root vegetables, 177
Stir-fried vegetable curry, 79
Sweet and spicy carrot pie with nut crust, 232
Vegetable burgers, 83
cashew nuts
Lentil & cashew nut roast with tomato sauce, 121
Spiced cream of pumpkin soup, 44
casserole, Eggplant & bean, 122
cassoulet, Mixed bean, 119
cauliflower
Stir-fried vegetable curry, 79
celeriac
Braised root vegetables with dried apricots, 188
Celeriac & spinach soup, 49
celery soup, Red lentil &, 47
cereal with fruit & nuts, Crunchy toasted, 26
cheddar cheese
Chilli bean & polenta bake, 126
Eggs florentine, 36
Lentil & cashew nut roast with tomato sauce, 121
Mexican bean burritos, 73
cheese *see* blue cheese; cheddar cheese; fetta cheese; goat's cheese; parmesan cheese; pecorino cheese; ricotta
cherry tomatoes
Beef niçoise salad, 132
Burghul & fish salad with lemon dressing, 148
Mediterranean lamb stew, 93
Thai chicken & green papaya salad, 140
chicken
Aromatic chicken with couscous, 102
Chicken & soba noodles, 58
Curried chicken and vegetables, 105
Mediterranean chicken, 101
Mexican chicken salad with salsa, 143
Moroccan braised chicken, 106
Spicy chicken tostadas, 70
Thai chicken & green papaya salad, 140
chickpeas
Aromatic chicken with couscous, 102
Bean & rice salad, 162
Beef & chickpea tagine, 89
Brown rice & chickpea pilaf, 201
Chickpea and pita salad, 77
Chilli bean & polenta bake, 126
Eggplant & bean casserole, 122
Falafel pitas, 74
Fruity Moroccan vegetable tagine, 112
Hummus with pita crisps, 207
Mediterranean lamb stew, 93
Moroccan braised chicken, 106
Persian-style couscous with roast vegetables, 197
Spaghetti with spicy tomato sauce, 61
Vegetarian pilaf, 76
chilli
Chilli bean & polenta bake, 126
Chilli con carne with cornbread, 90
Falafel pitas, 74
Mexican bean burritos, 73
Mexican chicken salad with salsa, 143
Mixed bean chilli soup, 57
Pork & bean chilli, 97
Red lentil & vegetable dal, 129
Speedy two-bean chilli, 118
Spicy chicken tostadas, 70
Thai chicken & green papaya salad, 140
Chinese beans *see* black beans
Chinese broccoli
Pork & plum stir-fry, 98
chorizo
Mexican rice with tomatoes & spices, 208
Christmas pudding, Fruity steamed, 228
cinnamon
Banana cinnamon muffins, 28
Cinnamon French toast with sautéed apples, 35
coleslaw
Crunchy nut coleslaw, 182
Thai-style beef sandwich with coleslaw, 80
coriander
Beef & chickpea tagine, 89
Burghul & fish salad with lemon dressing, 148
Mexican rice with tomatoes & spices, 208
Mixed bean chilli soup, 57
Salsa, 143
Spiced barley & corn, 187
Thai-style beef sandwich with coleslaw, 80
corn
Caribbean vegetable stew, 115
Chilli con carne with cornbread, 90
Corn & wholegrain wheat salad, 155
Mexican bean burritos, 73
Mexican rice with tomatoes & spices, 208
Pasta with roasted asparagus, 65
Pork & plum stir-fry, 98
Speedy two-bean chilli, 118
Spiced barley & corn, 187
cornbread, Chilli con carne with, 90
cottage cheese
Herbed eggplant lasagne, 116
couscous
Aromatic chicken with, 102
Baked couscous tomatoes, 181
Persian-style couscous with roast vegetables, 197
Crab & avocado salad, 147
Cream cheese icing, 239
cucumber
Barley & vegetable salad, 184
Burghul & fish salad with lemon dressing, 148
Corn & wholegrain wheat salad, 155
Middle Eastern bread salad, 166
curry
Curried chicken and vegetables, 105
Spiced cream of pumpkin soup, 44
Stir-fried vegetable curry, 79

D

dal, Red lentil & vegetable, 129
dates
Baked couscous tomatoes, 181
Boiled fruit cake, 240
Fruity steamed Christmas pudding, 228
Persian-style couscous with roast vegetables, 197
dips
Eggplant & tahini, 202
White bean garlic, 203
dressing
Lemon, 148
Mint, 169
Poppy seed, 170
Sesame, 149

E

eggplant
Eggplant & bean casserole, 122
Eggplant & tahini dip, 202
Herbed eggplant lasagne, 116
Red lentil & vegetable dal, 129
Warm grilled mixed vegetable salad, 191
eggs
Apricot hazelnut meringue cake, 217
Boiled fruit cake, 240
Breakfast bread pudding with berries, 29
Carrot & brazil nut cake, 235
Carrot & pineapple cake, 239
Cinnamon French toast with sautéed apples, 35
Corn & wholegrain wheat salad, 155
Eggs florentine, 36
Fruity steamed Christmas pudding, 228
Mixed greens frittata, 39
Spinach omelette & tomato mushroom sauce, 41
Sweet & spicy carrot pie with nut crust, 232
Tuscan-style baked polenta, 125
Vegetarian pilaf, 76
White bean salad with sesame dressing, 149
Egyptian brown beans, 15
English muffins, 36
English spinach
Eggs florentine, 36
Spinach, sweet potato & shiitake salad, 161
Wilted spinach salad with croutons, 165

F

Falafel pitas, 74
fava beans *see* broad beans
fennel
Chunky vegetable soup, 54
Fennel & potato with caramelised onions, 174
Herbed eggplant lasagne, 116
Mediterranean chicken, 101
Russian bean salad, 156
fetta cheese
Artichokes with lentils & beans, 111
Barley & vegetable salad, 184
fibre fill-up, 9
figs
Dried fruit, 211
Fresh fruit muesli, 25
Fruit & nut bread, 242
Persian-style lamb shanks with figs, 94
flageolet, 15
flathead
Burghul & fish salad with lemon dressing, 148
Focaccia with tomatoes & parsley, 69

French shallots
Braised root vegetables with dried apricots, 188
New England simmered beef, 86
Persian-style lamb shanks with figs, 94
Russian bean salad, 156
French toast with sautéed apples, Cinnamon, 35
frittata, Mixed greens, 39
Fruit & nut bread, 242
Fruit & nut-studded amaranth pudding, 214
fruit cake, Boiled, 240
fruit salad
Dried fruit, 211
Kiwi fruit & blueberry salad, 225
Melon salad with lime & yogurt sauce, 21
Winter fresh fruit salad, 22
ful medames, 15

G
garlic dip, White bean, 203
glycaemic index, 8
goat's cheese
Barley & vegetable salad, 184
Goat's cheese & watermelon pasta salad, 169
Pasta with roasted asparagus, 65
Pumpkin, lentil & goat's cheese salad, 150
golden syrup
Pear and rhubarb muffins, 31
grains, 12–13
see also under name eg rice
grapefruit
Roast pork & quinoa salad, 136
grapes
Melon salad with lime & yogurt sauce, 21
Greek-style yogurt
Baked couscous tomatoes, 181
Bircher muesli, 18
Turkey & mango salad, 139
green beans
Bean & rice salad, 162
Beef niçoise salad, 132
Chicken & soba noodles, 58
Lemony beans, 190
Mediterranean chicken, 101
Thai chicken & green papaya salad, 140
Vegetable salad with tuna, 144
Vegetarian pilaf, 76

H
haricot beans, 15
hazelnuts
Apricot hazelnut meringue cake, 217
Sweet & spicy carrot pie with nut crust, 232
honeydew melon
Melon salad with lime & yogurt sauce, 21
Hummus with pita crisps, 207

I, J
icing
Cream cheese, 239
Orange ricotta, 235

jalapeños
Mexican chicken salad with salsa, 143
Pork & bean chilli, 97
Spicy chicken tostadas, 70

K
kidney beans, 14, 15
Bean & rice salad, 162
Chilli bean & polenta bake, 126
Chilli con carne with cornbread, 90
Eggplant & bean casserole, 122
Mexican bean burritos, 73
Mexican chicken salad with salsa, 143
Speedy two-bean chilli, 118
Spicy chicken tostadas, 70
Kiwi fruit & blueberry salad, 225

L
lamb
Mediterranean lamb stew, 93
Mediterranean stuffed vegetables, 193
Persian-style lamb shanks with figs, 94
lasagne, Herbed eggplant, 116
leeks
Lentil & cashew nut roast with tomato sauce, 121
New England simmered beef, 86
legumes, 14–15
lemon
Burghul & fish salad with lemon dressing, 148
Lemony beans, 190
Tabouleh, 204
lentils
Artichokes with lentils & beans, 111
Lentil & cashew nut roast with tomato sauce, 121
Lentil salad with fried onions & rosemary, 153
Lentils with redcurrants, 194
Pan-fried fish with braised lentils, 100
Persian-style lamb shanks with figs, 94
Pumpkin, lentil & goat's cheese salad, 150
Red lentil and celery soup, 47
Red lentil & vegetable dal, 129
Spicy chicken tostadas, 70
Warm potato & lentil salad, 152
lettuce
Beef niçoise salad, 132
Crab & avocado salad, 147
Mexican chicken salad with salsa, 143
Middle Eastern bread salad, 166
lima beans
Mushroom and winter vegetable soup, 53
see also butterbeans
ling
Burghul & fish salad with lemon dressing, 148
linseeds
Multigrain seeded loaf, 249
Toasted oat & bran tea bread, 245

M
maize, 12
see also corn
mango salad, Turkey &, 139
Mediterranean chicken, 101
Mediterranean lamb stew, 93
Mediterranean roasted vegetable soup, 50
Mediterranean stuffed vegetables, 193
meringue cake, Apricot hazelnut, 217
Mexican bean burritos, 73
Mexican chicken salad with salsa, 143
Mexican rice with tomatoes & spices, 208
Middle Eastern bread salad, 166
millet, 12
mint
Burghul & fish salad with lemon dressing, 148
Corn & wholegrain wheat salad, 155
Mint dressing, 169
Pumpkin, lentil & goat's cheese salad, 150
White bean garlic dip, 203
Moroccan braised chicken, 106
Moroccan vegetable tagine, Fruity, 112
muesli
Bircher, 18
Fresh fruit, 25
muffins
Banana cinnamon, 28
Carrot & apricot with pecans, 236
Pear and rhubarb, 31
mung bean sprouts
Pork & plum stir-fry, 98
mung beans, dried
Stir-fried vegetable curry, 79
mushrooms
Braised root vegetables with dried apricots, 188
Corn & wholegrain wheat salad, 155
Herbed eggplant lasagne, 116
Lentil & cashew nut roast with tomato sauce, 121
Mushroom & thyme toasts, 38
Mushroom and winter vegetable soup, 53
Pork & plum stir-fry, 98
Spinach omelette & tomato mushroom sauce, 41
Spinach, sweet potato & shiitake salad, 161
Tuscan-style baked polenta, 125
Warm grilled mixed vegetable salad, 191
Wilted spinach salad with croutons, 165

N
nectarines, 25
New England simmered beef, 86
noodles, Chicken & soba, 58
nuts *see* almonds; brazil nut; cashew nuts; hazelnuts; peanuts; pine nuts; pistachios; walnuts

O
oat bran
Banana cinnamon muffins, 28
Pear and rhubarb muffins, 31
oats, 12
Bircher muesli, 18
Crunchy toasted cereal with fruit & nuts, 26
Fresh fruit muesli, 25
Porridge with summer fruits, 32
Toasted oat & bran tea bread, 245
okra
Fruity Moroccan vegetable tagine, 112
Seafood gumbo, 109
olives
Beef niçoise salad, 132

Chickpea and pita salad, 77
Grilled polenta and tuna pizza, 66
Vegetable salad with tuna, 144
Warm grilled mixed vegetable salad, 191
Warm potato & lentil salad, 152
White bean salad with sesame dressing, 149
omelette, Spinach & tomato mushroom sauce, 41
onions
Fennel & potato with caramelised onions, 174
Lentil salad with fried onions & rosemary, 153
Mediterranean lamb stew, 93
see also red onions; spring onions
oranges
Caramelised orange compote, 227
Orange & rockmelon sorbet, 218
Orange ricotta icing, 235
Persian-style couscous with roast vegetables, 197
Sweet potato salad with orange dressing, 159
Winter fresh fruit salad, 22

P

papaya salad, Thai chicken & green, 140
parmesan cheese
Eggs florentine, 36
Focaccia with tomatoes & parsley, 69
Mixed greens frittata, 39
Pasta with roasted asparagus, 65
Spinach omelette & tomato mushroom sauce, 41
Tuscan-style baked polenta, 125
White beans & silverbeet, 198
parsley
Baked couscous tomatoes, 181
Crunchy nut coleslaw, 182
Focaccia with tomatoes & parsley, 69
Lentil salad with fried onions & rosemary, 153
Mushroom & thyme toasts, 38
Tabouleh, 204
Warm potato & lentil salad, 152
White bean garlic dip, 203
parsnips
Braised root vegetables with dried apricots, 188
Roast potatoes & root vegetables, 177
Stir-fried vegetable curry, 79
pasta
Beefy pasta salad, 135
Goat's cheese & watermelon pasta salad, 169
Herbed eggplant lasagne, 116
Pasta with roasted asparagus, 65
Spaghetti with artichokes & broad beans, 62
Spaghetti with spicy tomato sauce, 61
peaches
Dried fruit, 211
Fresh fruit muesli, 25
Lentils with redcurrants, 194
peanuts
Crunchy nut coleslaw, 182
Thai chicken & green papaya salad, 140
pearl barley
Barley & vegetable salad, 184
Spiced barley & corn, 187
pears, dried
Dried fruit, 211
Fruit & nut bread, 242
Pear and rhubarb muffins, 31
Roquefort & pear salad, 170
Winter fresh fruit salad, 22
peas
Mexican rice with tomatoes & spices, 208
Split pea & green pea soup, 48
Stir-fried vegetable curry, 79
Vegetable salad with tuna, 144
see also black-eyed peas
pecans
Carrot & apricot muffins with pecans, 236
Roquefort & pear salad, 170
Turkey & mango salad, 139
pecorino cheese
Spaghetti with spicy tomato sauce, 61
Persian-style couscous with roast vegetables, 197
Persian-style lamb shanks with figs, 94
persimmons, 25
pie with nut crust, Sweet & spicy carrot, 232
pilaf
Brown rice & chickpea, 201
Vegetarian 76
pine nuts
Baked couscous tomatoes, 181
Fresh fruit muesli, 25
Fruit & nut-studded amaranth pudding, 214
Goat's cheese & watermelon pasta salad, 169
pineapple
Carrot & pineapple cake, 239
Melon salad with lime & yogurt sauce, 21
Pineapple salad with almond brittle, 226
pinto beans, 15
pistachios
Pumpkin, lentil & goat's cheese salad, 150
pita breads
Chickpea and pita salad, 77
Falafel pitas, 74
Hummus with pita crisps, 207
Middle Eastern bread salad, 166
pizza, Grilled polenta and tuna, 66
plum stir-fry, Pork &, 98
polenta
Chilli bean & polenta bake, 126
Grilled polenta and tuna pizza, 66
Multigrain seeded loaf, 249
Tuscan-style baked polenta, 125
pomegranate seeds
Eggplant & tahini dip, 202
Poppy seed dressing, 170
pork
Pork & bean chilli, 97
Pork & plum stir-fry, 98
Roast pork & quinoa salad, 136
Porridge with summer fruits, 32
potatoes
Beef niçoise salad, 132
Chunky vegetable soup, 54
Curried chicken and vegetables, 105
Fennel & potato with caramelised onions, 174
Lentil salad with fried onions & rosemary, 153
Mediterranean roasted vegetable soup, 50
New England simmered beef, 86
Roasted potatoes & root vegetables, 177
Russian bean salad, 156
Stir-fried vegetable curry, 79
Vegetable salad with tuna, 144
Warm potato & lentil salad, 152
prosciutto
Goat's cheese & watermelon pasta salad, 169
prunes
Dried fruit, 211
Fruit & nut bread, 242
pulses, 14–15
pumpkin
Mixed bean cassoulet, 119
Persian-style couscous with roast vegetables, 197
Pumpkin, lentil & goat's cheese salad, 150
Roasted vegetables & butterbeans, 178
Spiced cream of pumpkin soup, 44
pumpkin seeds, 249

Q

quinoa, 13
Roast pork & quinoa salad, 136

R

radicchio
Warm grilled mixed vegetable salad, 191
radishes
Crunchy nut coleslaw, 182
Spicy chicken tostadas, 70
raspberries
Breakfast bread pudding with berries, 29
Porridge with summer fruits, 32
Raspberry & walnut cake, 241
Raspberry cream, 225
Summer pudding, 231
red cabbage
Falafel pitas, 74
red onions
Bean & rice salad, 162
Beefy pasta salad, 135
Brown rice & chickpea pilaf, 201
Roasted vegetables & butterbeans, 178
Salsa, 143
Sweet potato salad with orange dressing, 159
Warm grilled mixed vegetable salad, 191
White bean salad with sesame dressing, 149
Wilted spinach salad with croutons, 165
redcurrants, Lentils with, 194
relish, Beetroot and onion, 86
rhubarb muffins, Pear and rhubarb, 31
rice, 13
Bean & rice salad, 162
Brown rice & chickpea pilaf, 201
Mediterranean stuffed vegetables, 193
Mexican rice with tomatoes & spices, 208
ricotta
Grilled polenta and tuna pizza, 66
Herbed eggplant lasagne, 116
Hummus with pita crisps, 207
Mixed greens frittata, 39
Mushroom & thyme toasts, 38
Orange ricotta icing, 235
Speedy two-bean chilli, 118
rocket
Goat's cheese & watermelon pasta salad, 169
Pumpkin, lentil & goat's cheese salad, 150
Roast pork & quinoa salad, 136

Russian bean salad, 156
Sweet potato salad with orange dressing, 159
rockmelon
Melon salad with lime & yogurt sauce, 21
Orange & rockmelon sorbet, 218
rolled oats, 12, 13
Bircher muesli, 18
Crunchy toasted cereal with fruit & nuts, 26
Fresh fruit muesli, 25
Porridge with summer fruits, 32
Toasted oat & bran tea bread, 245
Roquefort & pear salad, 170
rosemary, Lentil salad with fried onions &, 153
Russian bean salad, 156
rye, 13

S

salad
Barley & vegetable salad, 184
Bean & rice, 162
Beef niçoise, 132
Beefy pasta, 135
Burghul & fish salad with lemon dressing, 148
Chickpea and pita, 77
Corn & wholegrain wheat, 155
Crab & avocado, 147
Goat's cheese & watermelon pasta, 169
Lentil salad with fried onions & rosemary, 153
Mexican chicken salad with salsa, 143
Middle Eastern bread, 166
Pumpkin, lentil & goat's cheese, 150
Roast pork & quinoa, 136
Roquefort & pear, 170
Russian bean, 156
Spinach, sweet potato & shiitake, 161
Sweet potato salad with orange dressing, 159
Thai chicken & green papaya, 140
Turkey & mango, 139
Vegetable with tuna, 144
Warm grilled mixed vegetable salad, 191
Warm potato & lentil, 152
White bean with sesame dressing, 149
Wilted spinach salad with croutons, 165
see also fruit salad
salad leaves
Lentils with redcurrants, 194
Roquefort & pear salad, 170
Salsa, 143
sandwich, Thai-style beef with coleslaw, 80
sauce, Tomato, 121
seafood
Burghul & fish salad with lemon dressing, 148
Crab & avocado salad, 147
Grilled polenta and tuna pizza, 66
Pan-fried fish with braised lentils, 108
Seafood gumbo, 109
Vegetable salad with tuna, 144
Sesame dressing, 149
shallots *see* French shallots
shrimp, dried
Thai chicken & green papaya salad, 140
silverbeet, White beans &, 198
snow peas
Pork & plum stir-fry, 98
soba noodles, Chicken &, 58
sorbet, Orange & rockmelon, 218
soup
Celeriac & spinach, 49
Chunky vegetable, 54
Mediterranean roasted vegetable, 50
Mixed bean chilli, 57
Mushroom and winter vegetable, 53
Red lentil and celery, 47
Spiced cream of pumpkin, 44
Split pea & green pea, 48
soybeans, 15
Russian bean salad, 156
spaghetti
Pasta with roasted asparagus, 65
Spaghetti with artichokes & broad beans, 62
Spaghetti with spicy tomato sauce, 61
spelt, 13
spinach
Beef niçoise salad, 132
Celeriac & spinach soup, 49
Mediterranean stuffed vegetables, 193
Seafood gumbo, 109
Spaghetti with spicy tomato sauce, 61
Spinach omelette & tomato mushroom sauce, 41
Turkey & mango salad, 139
see also English spinach
Split pea & green pea soup, 48
spring onions
Baked couscous tomatoes, 181
Beetroot and onion relish, 86
Burghul & fish salad with lemon dressing, 148
Crunchy nut coleslaw, 182
Middle Eastern bread salad, 166
Spiced barley & corn, 187
Split pea & green pea soup, 48
Tabouleh, 204
Warm potato & lentil salad, 152
star anise
Winter fresh fruit salad, 22
stew
Caribbean vegetable, 115
Mediterranean lamb, 93
stir-fries
Pork & plum, 98
Stir-fried vegetable curry, 79
sugar snap peas
Aromatic chicken with couscous, 102
sultanas & brandy, Baked apples with, 221
Summer pudding, 231
sunflower seeds
Crunchy toasted cereal with fruit & nuts, 26
Fresh fruit muesli, 25
Multigrain seeded loaf, 249
swedes
Braised root vegetables with dried apricots, 188
Chunky vegetable soup, 54
Roasted potatoes & root vegetables, 177
sweet potatoes
Braised root vegetables with dried apricots, 188
Spinach, sweet potato & shiitake salad, 161
Sweet potato salad with orange dressing, 159

T

Tabouleh, 204
tahini dip, Eggplant &, 202
Thai chicken & green papaya salad, 140
Thai-style beef sandwich with coleslaw, 80
tomato passata
Spinach omelette & tomato mushroom sauce, 41
tomatoes
Aromatic chicken with couscous, 102
Baked couscous tomatoes, 181
Barley & vegetable salad, 184
Beef & chickpea tagine, 89
Beefy pasta salad, 135
Brown rice & chickpea pilaf, 201
Caribbean vegetable stew, 115
Chickpea and pita salad, 77
Chilli bean & polenta bake, 126
Chilli con carne with cornbread, 90
Chunky vegetable soup, 54
Crab & avocado salad, 147
Eggplant & bean casserole, 122
Focaccia with tomatoes & parsley, 69
Fruity Moroccan vegetable tagine, 112
Grilled polenta and tuna pizza, 66
Herbed eggplant lasagne, 116
Lentil salad with fried onions & rosemary, 153
Mediterranean roasted vegetable soup, 50
Mediterranean stuffed vegetables, 193
Mexican rice with tomatoes & spices, 208
Middle Eastern bread salad, 166
Mixed bean cassoulet, 119
Mixed bean chilli soup, 57
Moroccan braised chicken, 106
Persian-style lamb shanks with figs, 94
Pork & bean chilli, 97
Russian bean salad, 156
Salsa, 143
Seafood gumbo, 109
Spaghetti with spicy tomato sauce, 61
Speedy two-bean chilli, 118
Spiced barley & corn, 187
Spicy chicken tostadas, 70
Tabouleh, 204
Tomato sauce, 121
Vegetable salad with tuna, 144
White bean salad with sesame dressing, 149
see also cherry tomatoes
tortillas
Mexican bean burritos, 73
Mexican chicken salad with salsa, 143
Mexican rice with tomatoes & spices, 208
Spicy chicken tostadas, 70
tostadas, Spicy chicken, 70
tuna
Grilled polenta and tuna pizza, 66
Vegetable salad with tuna, 144
Turkey & mango salad, 139
turnips
Braised root vegetables with dried apricots, 188
New England simmered beef, 86
Roasted potatoes & root vegetables, 177
Tuscan-style baked polenta, 125

V

Vegetable burgers, 83
Vegetable salad with tuna, 144
Vegetarian pilaf, 76

W

walnuts
- Carrot & pineapple cake, 239
- Corn & wholegrain wheat salad, 155
- Crab & avocado salad, 147
- Pasta with roasted asparagus, 65
- Raspberry & walnut cake, 241
- Roquefort & pear salad, 170
- Spinach, sweet potato & shiitake salad, 161
- Sweet & spicy carrot pie with nut crust, 232

watermelon
- Goat's cheese & watermelon pasta salad, 169
- Melon salad with lime & yogurt sauce, 21

wheat, 13

wheat bran
- Toasted oat & bran tea bread, 245

wheat germ
- Crunchy toasted cereal with fruit & nuts, 26
- White bean salad with sesame dressing, 149

wholegrain wheat salad, Corn &, 155

wholemeal bread, Quick, 246

witlof
- Goat's cheese & watermelon pasta salad, 169
- Roquefort & pear salad, 170

Y

yellow squash
- Persian-style couscous with roast vegetables, 197

yogurt
- Baked couscous tomatoes, 181
- Bircher muesli, 18
- Crunchy nut coleslaw, 182
- Dried fruit, 211
- Melon salad with lime & yogurt sauce, 21
- Porridge with summer fruits, 32
- Toasted oat & bran tea bread, 245
- Turkey & mango salad, 139
- Yogurt cream, 226

Z

zucchini
- Aromatic chicken with couscous, 102
- Mediterranean lamb stew, 93
- Mediterranean stuffed vegetables, 193
- Persian-style lamb shanks with figs, 94
- Roasted vegetables & butterbeans, 178
- Warm grilled mixed vegetable salad, 191

Weights and measures

Australian metric cup and spoon measurements have been used throughout this book: 1 cup = 250 ml; 1 tablespoon = 20 ml and 1 teaspoon = 5 ml. If using the smaller imperial cup and spoon measures (where 1 cup = 235 ml and 1 tablespoon = 15 ml), some adjustments may need to be made. A small variation in the weight or volume of most ingredients is unlikely to adversely affect a recipe. The exceptions are yeast, baking powder and bicarbonate of soda (baking soda). For these ingredients adjust the recipe accordingly. All cup and spoon measures are level, unless stated otherwise. Ingredients are generally listed by their weight or volume with cup measurements given for convenience, unless the conversion is imperfect, whereby the ingredients are listed by weight or volume only.

Sometimes conversions within a recipe are not exact but are the closest conversion that is a suitable measurement for each system. Use either the metric or the imperial measurements; do not mix the two systems.

Can sizes

Can sizes vary between countries and manufacturers; if the stated size is unavailable, use the nearest equivalent. Here are the metric and imperial measurements for can sizes used in this book: 225 g = 8 oz; 300 g = 10 oz; 350 g = 12 oz; 400/410 g = 14 oz = 398 ml/410 ml; 425 g = 15 oz = 540 ml; 800 g = 28 oz = 796 ml.

Nutritional analysis

Each recipe is accompanied by a nutrient profile showing kilojoules (kJ), calories (kcal), protein, fat (including saturated fat), carbohydrate (including sugars), fibre and sodium. Serving suggestions, garnishes and optional ingredients are not included in the nutritional analysis. For the recipe analysis we used FoodWorks ® based on Australian and New Zealand food composition data. In line with current nutritional recommendations, use salt-reduced stock and soy sauce wherever possible.

Alternative terms and substitutes

broad beans fava beans

butterbeans lima beans

capsicum sweet pepper, bell pepper

coriander cilantro

corn cob mealie/miele

crisp fried noodles 2-minute noodles (do not use the sachet)

eggplant aubergine, brinjal

English spinach baby spinach; not the heavily veined, thick-leafed vegetable sold as spinach or silver beet

filo phyllo

fish substitutes for blue-eyed cod, bream, ling, snapper, flathead, use any firm white-fleshed fish such as cod, hake or kabeljou

fresh shiitake mushrooms rehydrated dried shiitake mushrooms

kecap manis sweet soy sauce

kiwi fruit kiwis

Lebanese cucumber Mediterranean cucumber, short cucumber

low-fat milk 1% milk

oat porridge oatmeal

oregano oreganum

papaya pawpaw

passionfruit granadilla

rice and corn fusilli wheat fusilli

rockmelon spanspek, cantaloupe

self-raising flour self-rising flour

semi-dried tomatoes sun-dried tomatoes

silver beet Swiss chard, often sold as spinach

Swiss brown mushrooms brown mushrooms

telegraph cucumber English cucumber, long cucumber

vanilla extract vanilla essence

Vietnamese mint mint or combination of cilantro and mint

wholemeal whole-wheat

witlof witloof, Belgian endive

zucchini baby marrow, courgette

High Fibre Cookbook

Consultant Suzie Ferrie, Advanced Accredited Practising Dietitian
Editor Jacqueline Blanchard
Design Concept and Senior Designer Donna Heldon
Designer Susanne Geppert
Nutritional Analysis Toni Gumley
Proofreader Susan McCreery
Indexer Diane Harriman
Senior Production Controller Monique Tesoriero
Editorial Project Manager General Books Deborah Nixon

READER'S DIGEST GENERAL BOOKS
Editorial Director Elaine Russell
Managing Editor Rosemary McDonald
Art Director Carole Orbell

CREDITS

Front cover, back cover (*background, top and centre insets*), pages 2, 4, 7, 11, 13, 15, 19, 23, 30, 33, 63, 76, 88, 92, 99, 110, 117, 137, 138, 141, 151, 163, 164, 168, 171, 185, 186, 200, 205, 215, 216
Photographer Ian Hofstetter, **Stylist** Trish Heagerty,
Food preparation Wendy Quisumbing

All images except the following are the copyright of Reader's Digest.
ENDPAPERS Shutterstock; 9 Shutterstock; 12 *left, all:* Shutterstock; *right, top to bottom:* Shutterstock, iStockPhoto, Shutterstock; 13 *left, top to bottom:* Shutterstock, iStockPhoto; *right, top to bottom:* iStockPhoto, Shutterstock, Shutterstock; 14 *left:* Shutterstock; *right, top to bottom:* iStockPhoto, iStockPhoto, iStockPhoto, Shutterstock; 15 *left, all:* iStockPhoto; *right, top to bottom:* Shutterstock, iStockPhoto, Shutterstock, Shutterstock; 16–17 Shutterstock; 42–43 Shutterstock; 84–85 Shutterstock; 130–131 Shutterstock; 172–173 Shutterstock; 212–213 Shutterstock.

High Fibre Cookbook contains some material first published in the following Reader's Digest books:
30 minutes a day to a healthy heart; Baking with love; Beat high blood pressure; Cook smart for a healthy heart; Diabetes cookbook; Eat well live well: Beautiful baking; Eat well live well: Eggs, milk & cheese; Eat well live well: Fresh fruit & desserts; Eat well live well: Poultry; Eat well stay well; Everyday arthritis solutions; Fight back with food; Healthy one-dish cooking; Midweek meals made easy; Super salads; Vegetables for vitality

FRONT COVER: *Pumpkin, lentil & goat's cheese salad, page 150*
BACK COVER: background *Pear & rhubarb muffins, page 31;* insets top to bottom *Pear & rhubarb muffins, page 31; Herbed eggplant lasagne, page 116; Baked apples with sultanas & brandy, page 221*
PAGE 2: *Fruit & nut-studded amaranth pudding, page 214*
PAGE 4: *Mediterranean lamb stew, page 93*
PAGE 7: *Spaghetti with artichokes & broad beans, page 62*

High Fibre Cookbook is published by
Reader's Digest (Australia) Pty Limited
80 Bay Street, Ultimo NSW 2007
www.readersdigest.com.au
www.readersdigest.co.nz
www.readersdigest.co.za
www.rd.com; www.readersdigest.ca

First published 2011.

National Library of Australia Cataloguing-in-Publication entry

Title: High Fibre Cookbook.
ISBN: 978-1-921743-95-5 (hbk)
978-1-921743-96-2 (pbk)
Notes: Includes index.
Subjects: Cooking.
High-fibre diet--Recipes.
Fibre in human nutrition.
Other Authors/Contributors: Reader's Digest (Australia)
Dewey Number: 641.5637

Prepress by Sinnott Bros, Sydney
Printed and bound by Leo Paper Products, China

We are interested in receiving your comments on the contents of this book. Write to:
The Editor, General Books Editorial,
Reader's Digest (Australia) Pty Limited,
GPO Box 4353, Sydney, NSW 2001,
or email us at bookeditors.au@readersdigest.com

To order additional copies of *High Fibre Cookbook*, please contact us as follows:
www.readersdigest.com.au, 1300 300 030 (Australia);
www.readersdigest.co.nz, 0800 400 060 (New Zealand);
www.readersdigest.co.za, 0800 980 572 (South Africa)
or email us at customerservice@readersdigest.com.au

NOTE TO READERS

The information in this book should not be substituted for, or used to alter, medical therapy without your doctor's advice. For a specific health problem or dietary concern, consult your doctor for guidance.

Concept code: AU 0739/IC
Product codes: 041-4408 (hbk), 041-4409 (pbk)

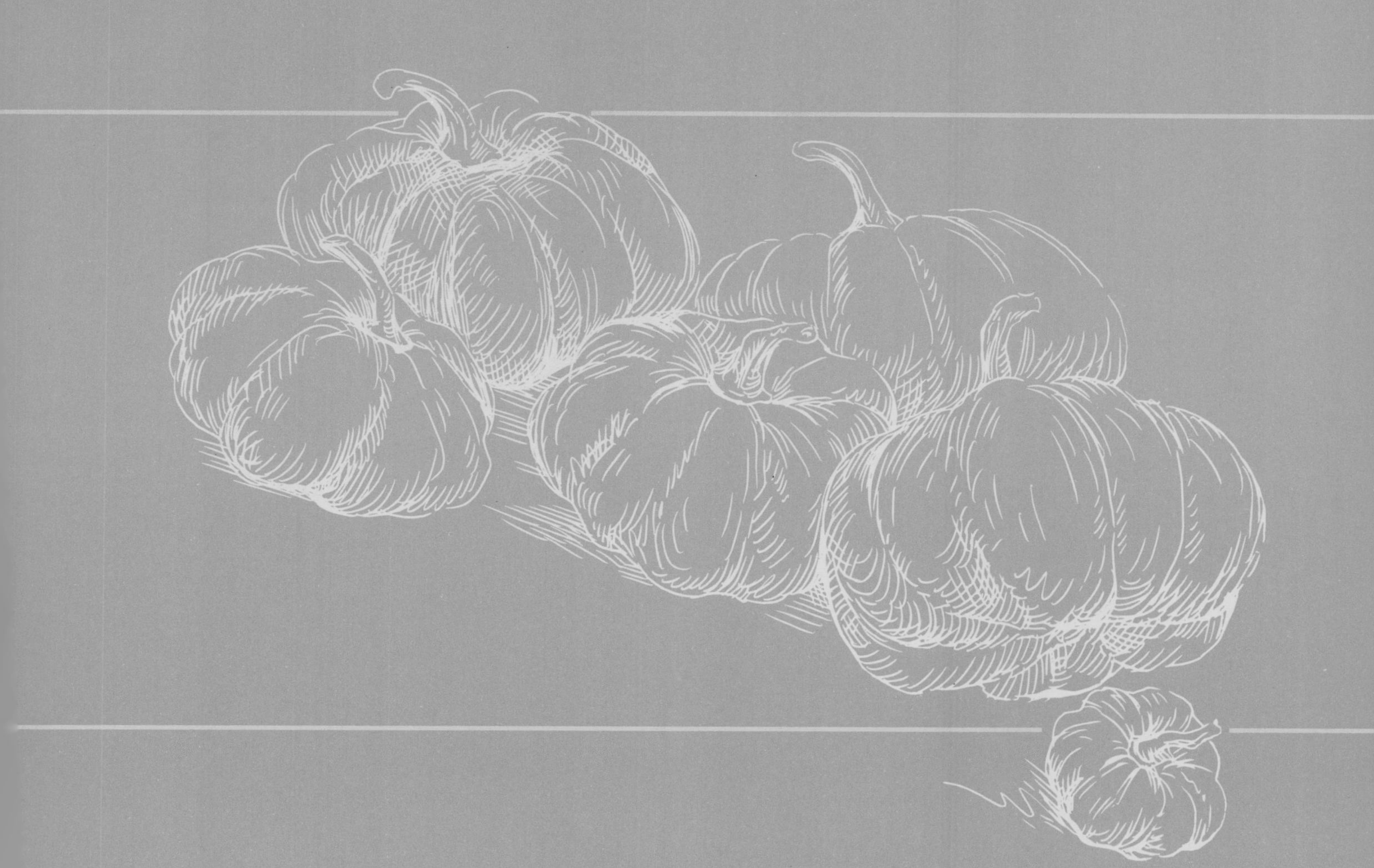